THE ART OF SOCIAL SELF-PROMOTION

A Satire on How to Become the Most Popular Woman You Know

Kathryn Latour

Illustrations by Iris Latour

PAGE PUBLISHING
Conneaut Lake, PA

First originally published by Page Publishing 2022

ISBN 978-1-6624-4227-8 (pbk)
ISBN 978-1-6624-4228-5 (digital)

Printed in the United States of America

CONTENTS

PREFACE NUMBER 1
Why You Need This Book

There are many people skilled in a particular area, often the result of years of study, practice, or some other form of hard work. We all recognize the effort that it takes to become a brilliant surgeon, a concert violinist, or the CEO of a large company. However, take two people with the same education and equal talent. Why does one achieve celebrity status and the other does not?

Let's take the film industry as a case in point. We have all seen aspiring stars acting in community theater who are as talented—in many cases more talented—than certain famous movie stars we could name. You know the movie stars I'm talking about. We go to their movies mostly because they make so many of them. Due to the law of averages, we will occasionally find ourselves watching some of their mediocre performances almost against our will, not because we are impressed with their acting skills. How have they achieved stardom with obviously so little acting ability? Sure, luck plays a part. Moreover, good looks must be acknowledged as often tipping the balance.

But—and I cannot overstate this—there is something else that the acting profession does very well and which makes all the difference.

Actors have managers and agents who know how to promote them.

I would bet good money on the fact that the bigger the star, the better the agent. It seems that the acting talent of the celebrity is of far less importance in this equation. A few other industries such as music, sports, and politics also routinely employ promoters to maneuver their careers and find them work.

What about the rest of us who have no managers? What are we supposed to do?

The answer is simple. We need to become our own managers. We need to learn the fine art of self-promotion. "This is all well and good," you say, "when it comes to my career. Self-promotion can achieve career advancement and just makes good economic sense." While it is true that women (and, okay, even men) can use the skills in this book to help them succeed in their profession, the real value of this book is in helping women navigate the social seas to become socially popular.

I am not talking about high school popularity where your main concern was whether people actually *liked* you. I'm not talking about the *mean girl* type of popularity either, where popularity was based on intimidation. With high school behind you, you need to catch the vision of a deeper, more satisfying, celebrity-making popularity, where everyone in your community knows who you are and regards you as the most accomplished person they know.

See yourself as the most poised, the most accomplished, and the most talented woman in your wide circle of acquaintances. Without question, your children are more confident, beautiful, and smarter than anyone else's are. Your husband is the most charismatic, brilliant, accomplished man anyone knows.

In time, because of your efforts at self-promotion, you and your family will become the standard to which everyone else aspires but cannot seem to achieve. And the best part is that you will do this without actually becoming smarter, more talented, or more accomplished! It is all about creating the illusion. Prepare yourself to become a master of friendly deception.

PREFACE NUMBER 2
Why I Needed to Write This Book

Now that you have read my fake reasons for wanting to read this book, I'll give it to you straight. I really hate these types of women, the type of women this book is teaching you to become.

There. I said it.

These women don't just think they are better than the rest of us. They *know it*. It sickens me. The worst part of it is this: It's as if they have memorized this book cover to cover because they have learned not to ever show their faults, they groom "perfect" snobbish children, and they greedily suck up every chair opportunity known to man. *Finagle* is their watchword.

They are social finaglers.

I truly have met social climbers like this. Boy, could I tell you some true stories! I won't, though, mostly because I don't want to be sued. Also, because some of these women think of me as their friend. I'm not sure why they do since they do everything in their power to keep me socially distanced in all the ways you are about to learn. But still, I suppose it's better not to purposely make enemies.

Some are so successful at their own social promoting, it's difficult for me to put my finger on why I detest them so. Maybe it's because they say they want to be friends to my face. But then they do not do any of the normal things one expects of someone who really wants friendship. That is they never have personal one-on-one conversations about what a tough time their son is having in math, or what their husband did to annoy them yesterday, or something funny that happened in the market. No. They float above me in their little perfect lives as if everything breezed by them without incident or anecdote. And I am convinced they secretly enjoy making me feel little by comparison.

They have created the perfect illusion of perfection.

They never admit to error either. I mean they do hold themselves to an incredibly high standard—at least in public. But any *faux pas*—even those committed on purpose—is blamed on someone else every time. Or they petition the offended one with flowers and a whole story about how it was just a misunderstanding. (I am actually clenching my teeth together at the moment to keep from throwing up all over my computer.)

It is so unfair. That is what bugs me the most. Everyone has skills and abilities, and many fine people can be great chair-people if only given the chance. Most of us have tremendous children and capable, even charming, spouses. In short, if we are not the most impressive woman we know, it is probably because we allow our humanness to show, or we are never given the opportunity to shine. Or that we occasionally slip up and have to apologize.

And that is how it should be.

We should interact with each other in a friendly, friend-inducing manner. We should confess to error at times, especially if we offended someone. We should invite families to our homes simply to draw closer to them, not for any social agenda. We should name our children beautiful family names that we actually like, not those that will socially elevate them.

I could go on and on.

So read my book, if you must, but read it only for entertainment. It was cheaper for me to publish this than undergo a lifetime of anger management. And know this: if you take any portion of this book seriously, my wallet will thank you, but I will not. You will know you have succeeded when you realize that *if I actually knew you, I would despise, even loathe, the socially self-promoted you.*

SECTION 1
Use Your Committee to Elevate Your Status

1.   Become the World's Worst Volunteer...on Purpose

We all have twenty-four hours in the day. There are people who can function on three to four hours of sleep a night, and I say they have no excuse for not finding a cure for cancer. The rest of us have an excuse because we need more sleep than that. (Since you are now thinking of yourself as the most accomplished woman you know, you will readily agree that the need for sleep is the only thing holding you back from curing cancer. And *you* could do it, mind you, in between making breakfast and cleaning up after dinner.)

By the time we ready ourselves for the day, feed our families, clean up, throw a load or two of laundry in, and head for our paid job (if we have one), our days are full. Even if we have no outside-the-home work, between running kids to lessons and other errands, who has time to volunteer for extra jobs? You do. Let me say that again.

You do.

And here is how. You volunteer for any run-of-the-mill one-man job for your church, PTA, or community and then turn it into a fabulous committee with you as its head. You give your committee a cool and trendy name (clever acronyms are especially good) and generate an official-sounding mission statement. You make it sound as though your committee is important enough to solve world hunger, even if what you volunteered for is only the middle school PTA volunteer librarian (which, as those of us who have done it know, is actually a vital underappreciated calling.)

For example, if your volunteer job is the abovementioned librarian, your organization could have the cool name of MAI (pronounced *may*), which, in our hypothetical, stands for mothers against illiteracy. Your mission statement could be something like "MAI is an organization dedicated to assuring that all children have access to inspiring literature to facilitate literacy."

Wouldn't you want to be involved in such a vital committee if someone asked you to come on board?

The next step is to call everyone you know to be on the committee. The more people, the better. At this point, think of yourself as a spin doctor. You paint a picture to your friends of how necessary this committee is to the community and how, together, you are going to revamp the old system, bring real and much-needed change to how it's been done before, and change the world one little step at a time.

Because—make no mistake about it—when you are done with your self-promoting, that is exactly what everyone will believe you can do. Bear in mind, this will initially take a few hours on the phone, and you will have to stroke the egos of all the women you call, relating stories (either actual or pretended) you have heard about their fabulous abilities.

This may sound like a lot of work, but keep in mind three things.

First, this will save you hours of time slogging through what would have been a solitary volunteer job with practically no reward or recognition.

Second, it will be infinitely more fun to have all your friends help you with this task and to have them stroke *your* ego about how brilliant *you* are for creating this fun committee while they are doing your work for you.

Third, your ultimate goal is to have your name be automatically associated with a leader of organizations. So tough it up and put some time into this. The more times you head an organization, the less time it will take you to convince others to help because your reputation for achieving something worthwhile will hereafter precede all your future requests for help.

Let us assume that you spend ten minutes each talking to six friends and get four of them to commit. First, consider this a huge success. You now have a posse. Second, you have only spent one hour, which is anyway a reasonable weekly time commitment for a volunteer job. And here comes the beauty part. After this initial one-hour investment (during which you get to chat with friends you might have called anyway just for aimless chatting), all you have to do is set up a regular meeting once a month to discuss goals and progress. You won't actually have to do any of the one-hour shifts of real work.

That is what your committee does. It is their very purpose.

Oh, you might have to sign yourself up for a shift occasionally, but after ten minutes or so of real work, you make it a point to pull aside the employee who is supervising volunteer efforts, Ms. X, and engage her in a serious discussion regarding your committee's goals.

Better yet, call Ms. X before your shift starts to ask if it would be possible to make a small presentation about your committee's goals while you are there. The employee will be flattered to think that anyone would consider an underpaid underappreciated employee worthy enough to schedule a meeting with. During your presentation, you make sure to stroke the ego of Ms. X for performing the herculean and unappreciated task of (fill in the blank with your committee's mission statement).

She will not only feel extremely valuable to her organization but will feel as though a great weight has been lifted from her shoulders because in your presentation you will emphasize how your committee will take on the lion's share of her job description. She will be giddy with the possibility that she can personally take credit for all that your committee will accomplish. She will have visions of being rewarded for your efforts, even of getting a raise. You will notice the unmistakable but subtle film of sweat on her upper lip as she contemplates what this will mean to her career. Once you see that, you can congratulate yourself.

You have just won over an important ally without having to do any real work at all!

Quiz

Take this short quiz to see if you were paying attention. Please answer true or false.

a) Volunteering means doing real getting-your-hands-dirty-, in-the-trenches work.
b) You should always snub the employees over your volunteer work because you are obviously better than they are.
c) Give your committee a very clever name. You cannot call it the Committee.
d) Only call important people to be on your committee.

Answers:

a) *False*
b) *False*
c) *True*
d) *False*

(If you missed more than one, go back and read chapter 1 because you are missing the whole point of this book already.)

2. Spin Doctoring 101

Let us go back to the mechanics of the meeting with the employee. You must arm yourself with more than your mission statement. You must consider this more than just a casual *tête-à-tête* with a low-level employee.

You must consider this the most important meeting of your social career.

After all, this is the beginning of your social makeover. You must treat it as the important first step it is. So in preparation for this all-important meeting, you call a meeting with your new committee. You tell them to have an important meeting with, in this case, the school. (You do not mention with whom your meeting is at the school. You want your committee to think it is with the highest possible person in charge.) You ask your committee to research the problem for which you formed the committee, even if you have already discussed this *ad nauseam* in previous meetings. You ask them to come to the next meeting prepared to discuss ways in which your committee will make a difference with—to continue with our example—the problem with illiteracy.

Your committee will scramble to come up with new and more-impressive ideas. They will come armed with statistics, examples from other school districts, programs instituted in the fifties before government defunding, anecdotal information from their children's experiences, and articles they have read in the National Geographic. You will be amazed at the level of research they do or at least they will after your first meeting when you suggest that your committee is in need of this sort of research. (It doesn't hurt to have a plant either, someone who you secretly appoint beforehand, someone you know will really run with this assignment and who will encourage the others by example.)

By the time you tell them about this meeting with Ms. X, they will realize your expectations, and they will step up. (Caveat: If they don't step up automatically, you may have to call on them individually to do this research, or you might have to do this research yourself the first time to show what you expect of them by example. Just remember to do anything it takes to make your meeting with the employee outstanding.)

Armed with these data, you set about making a formal presentation. Do not make charts or diagrams. Your presentation is not to be formal in its feel. In fact, it must have a casual air about it so that *Ms. X never knows what hit her.* It is only formal in that you will have committed all or most of the data to memory. You can bring a single page of statistics to bolster your presentation, but you should include only a few—nothing that will overwhelm your audience.

And you should also have prepared rebuttals to any arguments she may come up with, because even though she is already steadfastly on your side and wanting to make your program work, she has her reputation to think about. She cannot authorize a program that has been tried previously in another school but has failed. Anticipate that she will bring up similarities to other programs that may not have worked.

Here is the second key to developing your popularity.

Take credit for all the ideas you deliver.

It doesn't matter if every single library in the nation is doing a similar program. You will pitch the mission of your committee as if this were something you came up with all on your own. You will focus on the problem in your school and the urgent need for a solution that is unique to your situation. If Ms. X calls you on your lack of originality, you will simply underscore the differences between the program she is referencing and yours thusly, "While it is true that school old has done a literacy program before, our program focuses on illiteracy. The focus makes all the difference." If Ms. X cautions you that this program is similar to an old program that has not worked, you again underscore the differences. You will spin your idea as something new and vibrant. Knock down each of her arguments gently by emphasizing all the new and improved ideas your committee is willing to implement even if none of them are substantive.

Oh, and when you mention any idea your committee came up with, you state it *as if it sprang from your head* even if your committee has done every stinking bit of the work. You will use phrases such as "In my research," "I have found," or "I believe that," bringing the focus back on you. You must seem to be the genesis of all good ideas.

However, if Ms. X doesn't like one of the ideas, you quickly use your committee to distance yourself from it by throwing them under the bus, saying, "While I initially had my reservations, the committee felt this was a good idea because..." This approach has the additional effect of bolstering the idea without hanging yourself on a limb. Ms. X might not ultimately disagree if she thinks there are hundreds of committee members behind it. If she absolutely hates one of your ideas, allow her to give input, then tweak it according to her specifications so that she will have buy-in to your program. The bottom line is once she sees that you have marshaled potentially hundreds of person-hours for your new program, she will more than likely cease resisting and be lulled into the need for your program. Remember you have already curried her support in chapter 1.

Once you have made the presentation to the low-level employee, find a way to move up the chain of command until you find yourself in the office of the principal, pastor, mayor, or whoever the big guy is. Make sure the low-level employee talks you up so that the big guy is excited to meet with you. You may even welcome the employee into the big guy meeting so that she can give eager testimonials about your efforts to date.

You will give the big guy the same presentation you gave the low-level employee, but you will give it a broader spin. You need the big guy to see you as someone with vision, someone not content merely to shelve books as your predecessors have done, but someone who wants to use that school, congregation, or town as a model of what can happen when a community is recruited into working toward a grand goal.

Two things will happen as you move up the chain of command. First, you will be on a first-name basis with some pretty serious movers and shakers. New opportunities of a high order may come to you just because you now know these people, and they have been impressed with your vision.

Second, they may be in a position to do your committee a favor in some way. Everyone knows that, at times, there are visionaries who cannot make changes or implement their plans just because bureaucracy gets in the way. Big guys can move things through red tape when other avenues do not work, so make friends with these people and give them something of substance to think about while you are at it.

Your popularity is off and running!

Quiz

I have prepared another quiz to see if you were paying attention. Answer true or false.

a) Ask to meet with the employee in charge in order to make a huge formal presentation.
b) Call a committee meeting to come up with ideas for you for the presentation.
c) Always give individuals on your committee credit for their ideas.
d) Move up the chain of command until you meet the big guy.

Answers:

a) *False*
b) *True*
c) *False*
d) *True*

(If you missed more than one—and especially if you missed C—go back and read chapter 2 because apparently, we are experiencing a failure to communicate.)

3. Oh, But That Was Your Idea

In your presentation with Ms. X and in future presentations to boards, the press (covered in a later chapter), and colleagues of any kind, you must remember one important point.

Never give credit to any other individual.

You must refer to your committee, however, because this makes you seem more important. You are the leader of an entire committee. It doesn't matter if your committee only has four (sometimes three) part-time members (one of whom brings her colicky baby and another who misses half of every meeting). If they are breathing and if they even showed up once, you will claim them as part of your committee and, therefore, a part of your popularity empire.

You will refer to your committee at all times as *my committee* or, even better, *a committee of many talented people*, emphasis always on *the many* not on *the talented*. The word *many* gives your audience the impression that you are the leader of a virtual nation of people while the word *talented* draws their attention toward the committee as the possible source of all your good ideas. You don't want that to accidentally happen. Saying *my committee* is likewise good because it gives the subtle message that all this is your doing. Your presentees will think you have done it all, but that you are graciously giving all credit to your committee. *How noble you will appear!*

But here, dear reader, you stop me and ask, "Why must you give your committee any credit at all?" Ahh, little grasshopper, watch and learn. It is because of two reasons. First, you do not want to alienate any member of your committee who may be in the audience or who are accidentally within earshot. Refusing to mention them by name will be overlooked if you offer a little crumb of appreciation by referring to them in the collective as talented, amazing, hardworking, etc. (If they are in the audience, take a moment to beam in their direction but still without mentioning their names. They will each know that you are secretly referring to them individually and that will invite them to be loyal to you forever.)

Second, you never want to appear egotistical. Even though you want your audience to remember your name and to associate only your name with this project, everyone hates a braggart. You want your audience to be impressed with your forward-thinking ambition, your keen leadership, and best of all, *your* hard work that has accomplished/will accomplish this herculean task almost single-handedly.

The borders of your popularity empire will enlarge as you are speaking because using this tactic will win over several members of the audience then and there!

Quiz

You are correct in recognizing that I am forcing you to take this short quiz to see if you were paying attention. Kindly answer true or false.

    a)   Often refer to the committee as *my committee* in order to bring the focus back to you.

    b)   It is okay to admit that your committee is small or doesn't really do much.

    c)   Do not brag but subtly take credit for your committee's efforts.

    Answers.

    a)   *True*
    b)   *False*
    c)   *True*

(If you missed any, you must have been asleep. Go back and read chapter 3 because the rest of the book is useless to you until you get this concept.)

4. Know What Is Going On. Sheesh!

Occasionally, you may find yourself in a situation where you are not the leader of a committee or organization. This is unavoidable because first, as amazing as you are, you simply will not have time or the ability to volunteer for every position. Second, there may be committees you are invited to join by an already-existing leader. In those cases, it is sometimes more advantageous for your popularity to be a member of a committee rather than decline the invitation just because you are not the leader. Third, you are, hopefully, involved in more than one hobby, occupation, social group, or volunteer organization. If not, you need to expand your areas of potential influence. When you find yourself in the back seat, how you handle this can either increase or decrease your popularity.

If you are in a committee but are not the leader, you should try your best to be an informed committee member. Whatever the mission of the committee, *the worst thing you can do for your popularity is to allow the leader to be completely in charge.* This does not mean that you should try to take over the meetings or try to get the leader deposed. In fact, doing anything that smacks of insubordination or disloyalty toward the leader only brands you as a troublemaker and detracts from your popularity. You don't want that.

Instead, you should research the mission of the committee thoroughly so that you can bring forward-thinking ideas to the meetings. (In fact, you might form a committee whose sole purpose is to research ideas for you to use in this other committee. Okay, maybe now I am being just a little ridiculous and taking my committee-forming idea a bit too far. I, however, do not believe you can go too far if you truly want to become the most popular leader you know. See also chapter 2 for a reminder to take credit for these ideas wherever you find them.) Either way, make sure you have several good ideas for any one meeting in case one of them does not meet the approval of the rest of the committee.

Follow all the ideas in chapter 2 in preparing to air these ideas. *You cannot afford to just throw out things off the cuff.*

In pitching your ideas, you have the ability to not only impress the rest of the committee members, but if your ideas sound well thought out, the committee leader may elect to put you in charge of implementing that particular idea. You, of course, will graciously accept this honor. (Remember to help her come up with that idea by alluding to the fact that you would be happy to implement your idea, if needed.) If you continue with this practice, the rest of the committee—if not the leader—will soon defer to you as the real leader of the group! Bingo! This is almost as good as being the actual leader as far as your sphere of influence is concerned.

This may sound to you like excellent advice for anyone on a committee. Shouldn't all committee members be doing regular research to benefit the committee's mission? Why, of course they should! I never said that these practices wouldn't help in other ways. The difference is that committee members who research just to profit the committee are shortsighted altruists. At the same time they are benefitting the committee's goal, they could be benefitting themselves as well. Poor, sad, sorry chumps.

Quiz

Are you ready for this short quiz to see if you were paying attention? Answer true or false.

a) If you are only a member of a committee, not the leader, do everything in your power to sabotage the leader's efforts.

b) It is fine to come to committee meetings without preparing anything to say. After all, you are not the leader. You have no agenda.

c) Take credit even if the ideas you voice are not your own.

d) Volunteer another member to implement the ideas you bring up.

Answers:

a) *False*
b) *False*
c) *True*
d) *False*

(If you missed any, shame on you. It is as if you don't believe that it takes real work to make you popular. Go back and read chapter 4.)

5. Speak for the Collective, Even if They Are Imaginary or Their Opinions Are Fictitious

We have already discussed the philosophy that your opinion by itself is not as strong as the opinion of a large collective. (See chapter 2.) It is true that mothers all over the world have heard the not-so-convincing argument from their child of "but so-and-so gets to go to that movie" as ample evidence that said child should be allowed to attend an inappropriate movie. Most mothers have the now-famous retort constantly at the ready. "If so-and-so jumped off the bridge, would you do it?" Let us hope this is not a persuasive argument when your child wields it against you. It is, however, a very effective weapon in your arsenal of popularity tools.

No one likes the feeling of standing alone against a group. It was not fun in high school when you were the only girl whose parents refused to let you have a prom dress that showed your new cleavage, and it is not fun now. But now, the tables have turned! You are not the one standing there alone in your high-necked formal.

Anytime you are in a position of giving your opinion, you must never stand alone.

Let us back up a bit and say you must always be *prepared* to give an opinion. Never pass up the opportunity to have your voice heard. Whether you are the leader of a group, a member of a committee, or an invited observer of another committee, you must have an opinion about something and you must be prepared to state it. It doesn't have to be your original idea (again, revisit chapter 2) as long as you have thought it through and give the impression that this view is shared by many, many others.

What if the opinion isn't actually one shared by others? Here is where slight prevarication comes into play.

Let us say that as a parent of budding teenagers, the PTA has invited you to a meeting where their aim is to increase attendance at middle school dances. You are not the PTA president, only a parent. Knowing the aim of the meeting days beforehand, you talk to your children and gather their insights, which may be that they don't like middle school dances because they don't serve any refreshments at them. You talk to your partner and get his or her opinion as well, even if it is only "Whatever the kids say is probably right."

Armed only with two opinions from people related to you, you can now bolster your opinion by saying, "I polled middle schoolers and their parents in my neighborhood. In their opinion, attendance is low because no refreshments are served at the dances." Never reveal who the opinion-makers are or that you are related to them or even know them personally. Add your opinion in agreement of theirs and then offer a solution. If committee members disagree with you, all you have to do is reiterate that it is not your opinion, but the opinion of an overwhelming number of people.

What if someone has the nerve to challenge you? What if you are asked to name names or tell exactly how many opinions you collected?

You still do not reveal that you only polled your family members. Doing so will reduce the impact of your statement unless your children happen to be movers and shakers in their sphere of influence: student body presidents, head cheerleaders, captains of sports teams, star performers. If any of your children is in one or more of those positions, you should state that "it was the opinion of ____, and ____, and ____ [give all the names of your children—without drawing attention to the fact that you are the children's mother—and the names of their best friends as well], but that as the _____ [fill in the blank using the position of prominence your children hold], they are in a position to know what a large number of other students feel."

Using this method not only shores up your opinion, but you elevate your standing in the community by being related by blood or friendship to one or more of these young movers and shakers. The reason you do not focus on your relationship to them is that you must treat your children like the celebrities they are. Stopping to make sure that everyone knows they are your children diminishes their star value and, therefore, makes your use of them circular. That is, you need to use only their names to reinforce your argument. If your children are not local celebrities in their own right, then the committee will believe that as your children, they are only parroting what you want them to say.

Your statement will go something like this: "It is the opinion of Bobby Latour, who, as you all know is the star quarterback of Ridgemont Middle School and who knows everyone, and his friends, Elvis Brown, student body president, and Teena Turning, head cheerleader, that refreshments at the dances would greatly improve turnout."

Using this tactic will usually silence the curious questioner. If it doesn't, or if your children have not risen to that status in the social ranks of your local schools, you must be prepared to say something evasive but convincing about who these people are who you polled. Being wholly evasive will rob you of any credibility you have gained so far, so err on the side of being overly convincing. Learn this phrase by heart: "I do not have a firm count of the many students and parents I polled, but it was sufficient to persuade me that this was an overarching concern among the student body in general."

It is a somewhat white lie since you, hopefully, do have a firm count on the number of children you have, but if you know that your children represent the opinions of some of their classmates, then the white lie becomes not only possible but probable truth.

Repeat after me. "I will not technically lie, but I will fervently spin whatever glimmer of truth I have into a convincing statement."

This must be your watch cry, your mantra, your *raison d'être* if you are to excel in the social scene because *it's all about turning fiction into fact, baby.*

Quiz

Let's just see how much you learned this time. Please answer true or false.

a) Always have an opinion to share at any time about anything.
b) You can use your family member's opinions to support your ideas.

c) Voice your opinion with supporting testimonials to back it up.
d) Never reveal your supportive sources unless it is advantageous.

Answers:

a) *True*
b) *True*
c) *True*
d) *True*

(I decided not to try to trick you by writing any falsehoods this time. I mean, you are having such a hard time as it is getting these answers right! Do you need to reread chapter 5?)

6. Once the Leader, Always the Leader

The opportunity to become the head of an important commit-tee will come eventually as you continue to put yourself forward, but for now, you must *create the illusion that you are important* and have previously been or currently are the head of many such committees. There is a fine line between outright lying and generating an aura of importance. You must not stoop to actual lying, but you must also never give the impression that you are someone people can question. This requires a great deal of finesse.

For instance, you must never say, "When I was the chairman of the board of the San Francisco Opera Company, we did x, y, and z." If it's not true, you cannot say it. People can easily research such a bald-faced lie. Everything is on the internet these days. But you can say, "In working with our renowned opera company in San Francisco, our leadership took these steps."

If you do this well, you will achieve two solid results. First, you will not give your audience any hard facts to trace. No one will know that it was not the San Francisco Opera Company but the burgeon-ing opera company of Podunk Community College that you assisted, not chaired. The illusion will be out there. It will, we hope, spread as a rumor that you were, in fact, the chair of the San Francisco Opera Company, and before you know it, your entire community will be impressed with your past leadership. Second, if you have been gracious with your fellow committee members, it will not occur to them to research your assertions. They will give you the benefit of the doubt. They will assume you are usually the head of whatever committee or board you have been on.

However, and third, if someone who you have not yet won over does decide to research your past accomplishment, she (it is almost always a petty, jealous woman) may ask you point-blank if you have really served as the chair of the San Francisco Opera Company. She will say this with a steely gaze, an edge to her voice, and a rigid smile as if she trying to be your confidant, not trip you up in a lie (which, of course, she is).

Do not waffle! Do not admit that you were never the chair!

Instead, you must keep the illusion alive by anticipating and preparing for this question by researching the San Francisco Opera Company. You must know who the chair is and be able to refer to him/her casually by name. (Let's say it is John Gunn.) Then you can truthfully state to this nervy individual that you did not have the honor of serving as chair of that organization, but you greatly admire John's leadership. Because you reference John Gunn readily and without hesitation, the social interloper will be convinced that you not only worked on the board of the San Francisco Opera Company but that you were John's right-hand man. You do not have to state the name of Podunk Community College and their sorry opera company. In fact, you *must* not in order to keep the rumor alive.

Do you see what else has just happened?

Because you do not deny the rumor completely but have given enough hard honesty, *your accuser will feel vindicated as if she has uncovered the real story.* It is unlikely that she will press you further. But if she peppers you with more questions, throw her a bone by saying something vague such as "The inner workings of opera are not as glamorous as most people think they are." Draw on your opera board experiences to enlighten her about how boring costuming budgets truly are to make your statement convincing. Be gracious. Put your hand on her arm as you offer to chat with her again so that she believes you sincerely wish to have a discussion with her sometime. Do not act in a hurry to deflect her or rush off. Doing so will only raise her suspicions that you have something to hide.

Summary

No quiz this time because you were doing so poorly at getting the answers right. Here are the all-important bullet points from chapter 6:

- Allude to your past leadership.
- Create the illusion that you once led a very important committee.

- Allow the rumors to persist if people confuse your actual past leadership with a more important one.
- Never divulge the truth of your past leadership but continue to reinforce the rumors.

7. Complaint Is a Perfectly Acceptable Competition-Squashing Tool

There may be times when you are not a member of a committee, but one of its members solicits your opinion about their performance. This may be because you are an interested party, such as a parent would be to the PTA leadership. Or you may be a new member of the committee and you are asked to give feedback as a recent outsider. Either situation is a golden opportunity to improve your popularity.

Never pass up the invitation to criticize another leader or another committee. (Actually, scratch that. You should never criticize another leader, only the committee. A leader might take your criticism personally, even if you follow all these other steps to a T.)

The first thing you must do is compliment the committee, even if they are doing a terrible job. Either you must find something to say about them personally or about their job performance that ingratiates you to them. *Then segue immediately into a mild attack on their performance.*

"Wait!" I can hear you say. "This can't possibly improve my popularity." Oh, but it can. If you object to their job performance without any malice in your voice and with confidence, it will elevate you to the level of expert, an expert who is merely dispensing much-needed wisdom.

And when giving your opinion, you must refer to your past or present leadership to bolster your implied leadership expertise. You do not have to contrast their poor performance with your excellent performance. Doing so only makes you seem petty. It is enough to refer to your leadership tenure in passing to remind everyone what a superior leader you are without having to state it. You will be seen as the consummate authority on the subject rather than as a catty has-been leader. People will be impressed with your humble refusal to compare your superior performance to their shoddy one.

Do not just mention your criticism in passing either. *You must flesh out your criticisms with exact examples of what they have done poorly* and then give the opinions of others to give credence to your criticisms (even if the opinions are fictitious or the people who have told you their opinions are imaginary—this is covered at length in chapter 5). A lengthy explanation about why their idea has not worked must follow along with a suggestion about what they could do better. You may also refer to other programs that are similar and have not been successful. Pull the Ms. X strategy from chapter 2. (Remember they have invited you to give feedback.)

If they come up to you later and ask why you were so critical, you innocently blink and gush as sincerely as you can. "Oh, I'm sorry. I thought you were asking for constructive feedback." Then you use this opportunity to emphasize your criticism by again saying, "When I said blah, blah, blah, it was not a criticism of you personally. The way you are handling this issue just isn't working, and I sincerely thought you would welcome my help, but I am sorry if I stepped on anyone's toes. It is your committee, and I have every confidence you will fix the issue beautifully."

Do you see the art of what you have just done? You have grabbed hold of a second opportunity to criticize, you have lauded yourself as the expert leader, you have positioned yourself as an altruist trying to help, and you have stroked their egos by giving them your vote of confidence. With one blow, you have reestablished yourself as the one and only true leader against whom this other committee will compare their leader, *and* you have done this without giving anyone room to complain about you!

Summary

Here are the most important points from chapter 7:

- Criticize the current leader's committee work.
- Flesh out your criticisms with examples.
- Suggest how she and the committee can improve.
- Criticize again, if possible.
- Express your confidence in her ability to do better.

8. Did You Honestly Think We Were Done Complaining?

If you are the previous chair, and the new chair of the committee asks you for your reaction to any point of her leadership, you must critique her publicly so that the new chair will believe that she stands alone in her way of doing things. She may have her entire committee behind her. She may have done her own research. In short, she may have done exactly what you did in your tenure as chair to support her own way of doing things. None of that matters when she asks you to give your opinion of the job she is doing because she is asking for it. *She is asking for it.*

You must never let that opportunity pass you by even if she is doing a far better job than you ever did. What do you do if she doesn't ask for your input? You simply raise your hand and say that you just have one small suggestion as a former chairperson. The opportunity is always there. Sometimes it is not offered, but you must always take it.

Find something—anything—to criticize, even if it is that she gives only two weeks' notice for meetings. (Who really cares?) Then as you give your opinion, you can state that two weeks is simply not enough notice for most people. When you were chair, your committee insisted that they needed a month's notice. In fact, this has been the norm for every committee you have ever been on. Then you must end your comments by stating what a gross inconvenience it is for you and your family to try to bend your busy schedule around a spontaneous meeting, whether it truly is an inconvenience or whether you had nothing else on the calendar that entire month. *Or even whether your committee was guilty of doing the exact same thing!* (Because it is the principle of the thing, darn it!)

And don't stop there.

The next time the chair asks for comments (or at the end of the very next meeting when she should ask for comments), raise your hand and *reiterate your criticism.* You should never reference that you have previously made the same complaint. Speak out as if this is the first time you have ever said anything on the subject. Flesh out all your same points in an even more elaborate fashion. The reason you will do this is that it is unlikely the first time you gave your criticism the new chair actually took your advice. Until she does, your complaint is still valid.

Not only will this technique remind her again that she is doing a poor job comparatively, but it will be an additional blight on her leadership for her to have asked for comments but then be too rigid, too proud, or too incompetent to implement them. The reality is that it may have been logistically impossible given the lack of time between the last meeting and this one to put your idea in place. Never mind about that. You cannot be bothered to worry about *why* she failed. Your duty is to remind everyone that she asked for or allowed the input of the former fabulous chairperson and then failed to implement it.

If she begins explaining, you allow her a few sentences, then you sweetly interrupt with "Oh, I'm sure it is very difficult to be in your position." This reminds everyone that you *were* in her position. The implication left unsaid but which everyone will think is that *you did a better job of it.*

After the second time of complaining, should you raise the issue again? Never! Doing it once makes you look savvy. Doing it twice underscores your competitor's incompetence. Raising the issue a third time reduces you to a petty woman who can't get her way. Once you have made your point twice, leave it. You will earn the admiration of all those around you who, like you, have seen the chinks in the new chairperson's armor. They will be unable to help comparing your two administrations, and in such a comparison, you will invariably win.

They will long for your return to leadership.

Now you may be asking, "How can pointing out someone else's flaws win me friends?" Give yourself a slap for letting that thought crease your forehead because *this book is not about making friends.* Didn't you read the preface to this book? That is not the aim of this book. For your punishment, go back to preface number one and reread what type of popularity we are talking about. I will wait.

*****

I am back now.

You should have just read, "I am not talking about high school popularity where your main concern was whether people *actually liked you.* I'm not talking about the *mean girl* type of popularity either, where popularity was based on intimidation. With high school behind you, you need to catch the vision of a deeper, more satisfying, celebrity-making popularity, where everyone in your community knows who you are and regards you as the most accomplished person they know."

Now do you see how complaining fits into your grand scheme? It is immaterial whether your words of complaint win you friends *in the short term.* Because everyone likes a winner, most people will confuse your leadership with friendship anyway, and you will have more "friends" than you know what to do with. (To understand why the word *friends* is in quotes, read the preface again and then give yourself another slap for forgetting that important concept.) The real benefit of your strategic whining is the shoring up of your reputation as the best leader anyone knows, the gold standard, the ultimate chairperson. That has to be worth the possibility of annoying a few people.

Summary

Here is my distilled brilliance from chapter 8:

- Criticize the current leader by drawing comparisons to your own fine leadership.
- Repeat the same criticism at the next meeting.
- If she tries to justify failure to implement your suggestion, agree that her job is difficult.
- You are not looking for friends.

9. Ye Shall Not Budge

At this point in your social career, you should begin to see yourself as someone a bit above your peers. You must never state it or act as though you know you are better because people who do that are snobs, and we will have none of that, but the reality is that you may now think it. You have earned the right to think of yourself as a cut above others in the leadership department. You have established yourself as a name, a reputation, a quasi-celebrity, a leader, and a force to be reckoned with. You have earned the right to insist that everyone involved with your committee honor the mission your committee is working hard to achieve.

(Having stated that, it does not mean that you are disagreeable, standoffish, or difficult to work with. You have a responsibility to appear to be the most magnanimous woman in the world. Your aura must give off calm, peace, comfort, and joy. You must give the impression that you are easy to work with and that attending a meeting you have called will be the most fun and rewarding experience of the day/week/month for those who you call to come. But let's get back to the real focus of this chapter.)

This means that if you have scheduled an event, and some other organization wishes to take advantage of this event to set up camp around the perimeters, *you say no.* Why? Because you will not tolerate any type of competition at your event. You need your event to stand alone and receive everyone's full attention. It cannot suffer the distraction of any other effort, no matter how worthwhile.

Let us say that in your role as assistant librarian, you are in charge of organizing a book faire, where students and parents can purchase books. This event promises to draw the bulk of the student body (four hundred students) plus some of their parents (another four hundred) for eight hundred people. That is a considerable group of people as Sally Sunshine, leader of the eight-year-old Girl Scout troop, realizes. All eight hundred are prime targets, a captive audience, if you will, for this cookie-selling hound and her cherubim.

The aforementioned Ms. Sunshine approaches you and pitches her idea of setting up shop outside the doors of the auditorium where your book faire will be operating over the course of three days. Although realistically speaking, customers may appreciate one-stop shopping, *you do not give in.* You cannot afford any social competition.

This event is your event.

You must not allow any other leader to appear anywhere near it for fear that others may mistakenly attribute some of the leadership, or success of the event, to her.

How can you dissuade her from this idea without making it appear that you are unreasonable? Customers are probably not going to buy fewer books because they have just purchased Girl Scout cookies, but this is the argument you will give. You will state that your committee has worked too hard for this event to fail simply because the customers' dollars were stretched too thin from buying cookies before they entered the book faire. You state that while you appreciate that the Girl Scouts are a worthwhile group that helps young girls to grow valuable life skills, you simply cannot accommodate the Girl Scouts' request and simultaneously honor the great responsibility you have of selling as many books as possible so that the book company will reward the school library with a large donation.

Then you hold fast.

Ms. Sunshine will push you by saying that all the girls are students there, and they have the right to set up whenever and wherever they wish. To that statement, you will simply say that you hope Ms. Sunshine will respect the large financial contribution the book company is sure to make to the library if sales are high enough. You say you trust that she will not detract from the focus of the book faire in any way that would jeopardize high sales.

If the tenacious Ms. Sunshine continues to pressure you, you will very sweetly state that you already have the approval of the principal to exclude any other activity on school property during the book faire. This means, of course, that you must have solicited this promise from the principal in anticipation of her request. You must resist the urge to tell Ms. Sunshine about the principal's promise before all your other arguments, or she will immediately run to the principal and pitch her case as if her cause is as important as yours is. This would be bad because you don't want the principal to view you as someone who causes others to waste his/her time. You must talk to Ms. Sunshine long enough until she is persuaded that standing in front of the grocery store might be her only recourse for public cookie sales.

This same ploy works when dealing with a troublesome worker on your committee. Occasionally, you will inherit a committee whose members are not of your choosing. You will have no control over picking these members and will not be able to handpick compliant workers whose only aim is to do your bidding. There may be those in the committee who actually believe you want their advice or, even worse, believe their opinion is as valid as is yours.

Let us say that the defiant Ms. Sunshine has assisted with the book faire since time immemorial and is a fixture on your newly acquired committee. Since she is also the Girl Scout leader, she believes that Girl Scouts should be used in all possible community efforts, including painting a backdrop for the book faire (if they won't be allowed to sell cookies). You hate her idea because it means that the lovely English garden setting you have tried to create with gazebos, tea tables, fine linens, and crumpets will be upstaged by a gaudy-and-far-too-ambitious rendition of Monet's Giverny Gardens. Here is how this conversation works.

> Ms. S will say, "I will assemble my Girl Scout troop to paint the backdrop for the book faire. We have been looking for a service project, and this will have the added benefit of helping them complete their art badge. This is perfect."
>
> You will say, "That is an excellent suggestion. I truly believe that service is a wonderful thing for children to do. However, I already have a well-renowned muralist who has agreed to take on this project." (It doesn't really matter if the muralist has agreed or if you have contacted this muralist or if you are even aware of a muralist living within your city limits. You must make Ms. S believe that you have a professional already com-

mitted. Even she will see that this is better than Girl Scouts.)

Ms. S will say, "Can't you cancel the muralist? [Okay, maybe the aggressive Ms. S doesn't see that your idea is better right away. You may have more work to do to convince her.] These Girl Scouts really need this opportunity. And my assistant leader is so talented. I'm sure she can help the girls do a fine job. Besides, as a matter of principle, shouldn't we use students whenever possible at a school function?"

You will say, "I love the idea of using the Girl Scouts. What a fabulous idea! I have been wondering who we could use to stand at the door and hand out the price lists. They will be so darling in little English maid outfits. It will be so charming and will be the perfect touch! Thank you for that suggestion. Can you organize a committee to put together English maid costumes?"

Not only have you deftly deflected Ms. Sunshine's silly idea, but you have also accomplished the following:

a) Complimented her
b) Given her credit for a creative idea that was actually yours
c) Handed off a task that makes her feel very responsible but will not ruin the book faire if she does it poorly
d) Accommodated her wishes to involve the Girl Scouts

You must "handle" Ms. S because it has not taken you very long to realize that not only is she opinionated, but her ideas and opinions are often bad ones. Once you have given her this area of nonessential responsibility, you can deflect her future offers by saying, "I'm sure you are overwhelmed with all you have to do with the English maid costumes. That is a huge contribution already. Let's have someone less vital be responsible for _____."

This is called win-win. Or in the world of social self-promotion (where we don't really care if anybody else wins because we are not interested in that type of popularity), that is called *you win.*

Summary

Here are the crucial bullet points you should have gleaned from chapter 9:

- Let nothing compete with your event.
- Deflect any well-meaning competitors with compliments and a different task.
- Assert that you have authority from above for your way of doing things.
- You win.

10. Meetings, Meetings, and Even More Meetings

There is an age-old tried-and-true rule of thumb for the socially ambitious. *You have to schedule and lead meetings.* Then do it again. Then do it again. Then…well, you get the idea. Meetings are the bread and butter of any leader wannabe because how can you possibly be regarded as a leader if you never lead anyone? Or, more aptly put, how can you possibly be regarded as a leader if you are never *seen* leading anyone?

You must provide a forum for others to see you in action as a leader. And you must do it often. You cannot just put your name on the chairperson's roster at your PTA, church, or community center and expect that people will notice. Your name will not jump out from the other seventy-five names.

Don't get me wrong. You should always put your name on every sign-up sheet that comes your way. Putting your name on any public document will help because somebody somewhere will eventually read it, and if she has heard of you already, she will notice your name. And, if your name is already out there in the community, it will serve to reinforce the image you have already created as a leader. But chances are your name on a list isn't going to add much to your social status. That is why you must schedule meetings.

Most serious business people hate going to meetings because it detracts from their real work. *They look upon meetings as a necessary evil.* They attend either because the meetings are mandatory or simply because meetings are the most efficient forum for giving feedback and/or learning what other departments in a company are doing.

But in your social popularity occupation, meetings are your real work.

You have to disabuse yourself of the notion that you will do anything other than run meetings. Ever. Your goal is to never be found in the trenches with the workers. If there is ever a task that needs getting done, no matter how minuscule, you will call a meeting—this is a meeting in addition to your regularly scheduled monthly meetings—in which you discuss the task, gather opinions, make assignments, and assign someone to take minutes of the assignments so that you can check up on the workers. It does not matter if doing the task yourself would only have taken you a half hour and, conversely, calling the meeting will take you an hour of calling, one hour of meeting time, and a half hour of follow-up and reporting. It is worth the waste of time to stand at the head of a meeting because *it is not about getting the task done. It is about creating your image.*

Let us look at the scenario where you decide not to call a meeting, and you just do the half hour of work instead. In all likelihood, no one will observe you doing the work, so you might not even get credit for your efforts. Even worse, someone might see you doing real work and revisit their impression of you. Instead of thinking of you as a leader, that person will carry away the image of you, sweaty-faced and bleary-eyed, working hard, just like any other nameless volunteer.

Do not stoop to doing actual work. Your calling is higher than that. Delegation must be your middle name.

"Wait!" you say. "If people hate meetings so much, won't I be the most hated woman on earth for calling so many of them?" Good question, but the answer is no. Not if you become adept at spinning the necessity of them. No matter what the task, you have to describe it in a way that makes your committee realize that this task is far too important just to entrust to one woman. You were forced to call a meeting to discuss the correct way to proceed. You needed the input of all these intelligent, creative, progressive-thinking women in order to forge ahead safely. You wanted assurances from your board that this task fell within the mandate of your committee. And you could not possibly just assign the task to someone without examining, in some detail as a committee, the best person for that task.

It helps to have other items on your agenda along with this one task. Even committee members who love working under your leadership have lives and will, at some point, come to resent you for calling unnecessary meetings if all you do is discuss one particular nonessential task for an hour.

So the first thing you must do when you call a meeting is either to restate the mission of the committee in an eloquent and inspiring manner or to express gratitude for the women of your committee who valiantly push this important mission forward through sheer force of will, talent, and great ability. If there is time, you may do both, but you should vary this message from meeting to meeting. During at least one meeting, you should name individual contributions in unique and glowing terms and allow the applause of fellow committee members to ring in their waiting ears.

Second, you should state the progress of your committee, if any progress is tangible enough to state. For example, you could state that the principal has just informed you that your book faire, in its second day, has already had more visitors than in any previous year. Or if no tangible progress is evident, you may state something intangible or unverifiable such as that renowned interior designer Gladys Bunkhead—who, as we all know, lives in our city and who had heard of our beautiful English garden setting from a neighbor—had glanced in for five minutes at closing on Tuesday night and found it completely charming. It helps if this happens to be true, but don't stand on ceremony. If it is only partly true, you may embellish the story for motivational purposes. (The truth happens to be that Gladys Bunkhead lives in the city. You know someone who lives on her street. That person thought Gladys Bunkhead would love the setting and invited her to pop in. Period.)

If one of the committee members says they were working on Tuesday at closing and did not see the celebrity, do not confess that Ms. Bunkhead's visit was only supposition. Instead, you may commiserate with her by saying, "It is unfortunate that she could only stay briefly. We will have to invite her to one of our committee meetings so that you can all meet her. Perhaps she can give us direction on our next faire."

Just saying this will appease the members, and you will never actually have to produce Ms. Bunkhead. In fact, you may promptly forget about Ms. Bunkhead until the following year when you will spin the story of her "visit" into something truly noteworthy. Or better yet, use that year to finagle an introduction to Ms. Bunkhead so that you can invite her to pay an actual visit to your worthy event. By now, your contact will view you as someone deserving of the attention of a local celebrity. If she doesn't, you will have a year to work on her.

Third—oh, but before we get to the third point, don't forget to assign someone to bring treats. In fact, assign several women to bring snacks so that you won't have to be the backup if someone forgets. *Remember, you should never put yourself in the position of having to do any real work, such as baking cookies.* It is always okay to have too many munchies if no one forgets. Having to bring refreshments also assures attendance since the assigned person will know that the missing treats will be noticed even if she herself is not missed.

Now here is the third point. Assemble a few far-distant projects to mention to the ladies to get them inspired for the future. These projects will act as the carrot before the donkey. Even if those projects are more of the same (next year's book faire), paint a picture of these projects as new and exciting. Emphasize the word "exciting." Say the words "fresh," or "innovative" repeatedly. Each committee member will lay awake at nights pondering her future involvement in those projects *with the hopes that you will choose her to be your right-hand man!*

Summary

Here are the crucial bullet points you should have gleaned in chapter 10:

- Call a meeting for any tiny reason.
- Create the feeling that you value your committee's input tremendously.
- In addition to the business at hand, state your gratitude for the committee or state the mission of the committee or state the progress of the committee.
- Assign treats.
- Briefly mention far-distant projects.

11. And You Thought We Were Done Talking about Meetings

We have been talking about committees for a while now, so much so, in fact, that you probably think it is not possible for you to do anything without one. That is only partially true.

If I've told you once, I've told you a thousand times how important it is to assemble, lead, and continue leading a committee for every single task you wish to accomplish.

However (and this is the big but), you should never prepare a meeting agenda without having planned in advance *exactly* what you want to have happen. That is, your committee is essential in completing tasks, but they are only moderately useful for giving you direction, purpose, ideas, or goals. You must have those firmly in place before the meeting starts. Of course, you will have a place in the agenda where you call for ideas about how to execute the plan, but when that time comes, you will already have done your homework.

You will not only have your own ideas, but you will have mentally implemented them into a systematic plan that will rarely incorporate anything that your committee has to say. Your committee cannot know this, of course. They must believe that they are contributing more to this enterprise than their labor. You cannot allow them to see that they are merely servants who must execute your grand scheme.

That is why you will make time for brainstorming in your meeting agenda. You will also ask a volunteer to take notes (or already have an appointed secretary in place) to capture the "distilled brilliance" that will come from your committee.

You will greet each idea enthusiastically with clasped hands and oohs and ahs. You will praise each member for her creative intelligence. But you will *never allow the committee to vote on any of the ideas.* Nor will you make any decision about these ideas in the meeting where you have just brainstormed. You will simply stop the brainstorming session at some point and say that you will synthesize all their ideas and present them in a cohesive plan at the next meeting.

What you will actually do at the next meeting is present the plan you have already generated (which may or may not, mostly not) have incorporated the ideas from the committee.

Because you have allowed the ladies to voice their opinions, they will believe they have been part of coming up with the plan. Be careful not to give individualized credit when you unveil the plan but praise them endlessly for their collective genius. They will instinctively take credit for it, and you will be their hero.

The same holds true if you are the head of a huge enterprise where many people are required to accomplish something on a grand scale. Let us suppose that you are in charge of an enormous renaissance fair intended as a fundraiser for a local charity. This is a far cry from the book faire you ran at the middle school where a national organization actually provided all the books, advertising, and setup ideas. All you had to do was organize a few women to man the cash register. (You led that book faire to greater heights than it had ever been before, but let's not get carried away—it was still just small potatoes.)

On the other hand, the upcoming mammoth production will require a huge venue, artisans to sell their wares, food vendors, street performers, music, advertising, and decorations. Fortunately, a sports club has donated its basketball court as the venue, but it must be transformed completely using volunteer labor. You call a committee and appoint competent people to manage each area of the production. One will be responsible for calling food vendors. One will solicit street performers and so forth. However, you have a problem. You realize it will be impossible for you to micromanage so many people in so many disciplines. You fear losing control. You are afraid that your committee members will start thinking on their own and make decisions that are counter to your overall design. What do you do?

What you do is call a meeting (naturally) at the onset *to define your vision of the production* and to voice your confidence in each "lieutenant" to carry out your directives. You won't actually state that they are merely lieutenants carrying out *your* directives. You will allow them to think that they have control over their area. In addition, you will allow them to function in their respective areas *as long as they do not deviate from your overall design.* You will express appreciation for their willingness to slave over their areas.

However, you will make it understood that they may not begin working on their assignment until they have provided a detailed account of what they propose to do. Then you will ask for constant feedback from each lieutenant starting with a written map of vendor/entertainment placement and ending with what color fabric will be used to drape the food tables. In the week of setup, you patrol the area, giving compliments but mostly asking innocent questions such as "Are you sure you want these food tables placed so close together?" or "Don't you think a less robust blue would work better draped here?" to let each lieutenant know you are carefully monitoring them. You do not do it in a heavy-handed manner. You simply ask questions as if you are brainstorming together. Then at the end of each day, when all the volunteers and committee members have left, you surreptitiously nudge tables, change fabrics, retie bows, and tweak the placement of banners until you are satisfied with the results.

The next morning, volunteers might notice that things were changed, and they will perhaps put them back, but after several days of this, *they will realize that a stronger force is at work and leave it.* If they complain to you, a lesser mortal would feign innocence and commiserate with them that someone dared tamper with their design. But not you. You will own your actions and reiterate your overarching scheme. You will sweetly but firmly state that they have failed to capture the vision of this grand enterprise. You ask them if they are confused about the plan and ask if they need help in executing it. You remind them of their voiced obligation to carry out the vision of this venture. You offer to assist them in getting it right. None of these volunteers will want to look incapable and will rush to assure you that, yes, they know the aim of the production, and, no, they do not require your assistance. They will feel as though they have let you down, not that you have micromanaged.

You do this with the decorators, the food vendors, the artisans, the advertisers—anyone and everyone who will touch this production. You must press forward until everyone knows that if what she is doing does not comport with the vision (a.k.a. *your vision,* but you must never pitch it as your vision or you will appear to be a little dictator) of the enterprise, *it will be struck down.* Like a benevolent parent, you will do it sweetly but firmly so that rather than thinking they accomplished something magnificent on their own, each volunteer will see how she was able to do well *only because you were there to guide her, to accept nothing less than perfection.*

Summary

You are so lucky I am taking pity on you by not requiring you to answer another quiz. To keep you pumped up, I am providing you with the essentials of chapter 11 below:

a)   Prepare for your meeting by generating an agenda.
b)   Allow for brainstorming in the meeting.
c)   Meetings are not democracies; do not vote on whether to implement any ideas.
d)   Craft a plan, irrespective of the suggestions, that you present at the next meeting.
e)   Ask for support for your vision.
f)   Micromanage every volunteer and remind them of their support of the vision.

12. Are We Seriously Still Talking about Meetings?

One last, but superb, point bears mentioning about meetings.

Meetings are the most useful tool you have in charting the waters of popularity.

You have seen how to manipulate them to suit your purposes, but I must discuss one more cunning use of meetings. What happens when you are in the middle of planning the citywide black-and-white ball fundraiser, and your daughter announces her engagement? Whatever you do, do not step down from your position. You can juggle all your responsibilities and throw a wedding for your daughter. In fact, plan a sailing trip to Turkey while you are at it. How? Call more lieutenants and assign them more responsibility. Call more volunteers to do the lieutenants' bidding. Call more meetings.

Whether you do a lick of work from this point forward, the important point is that your name stays on the door.

Now that we have that settled, the next point is to *never assume that your personal life and your volunteer life must remain separate.* The first place you begin merging the personal half with the scheming half of yourself is in your meetings. Use the members of your committee as an extension of your social life. The first reason you do this is that you have very few real friends. Your poor daughter will have pitifully few guests at her wedding if she is relying on your true friends to populate it. The second reason—and the point of this whole social promotion endeavor—is to spread goodwill.

I don't think I am too far off the mark when I state that everyone's favorite social gathering is the wedding reception of a prominent individual's family member: free food and drink, schmoozing with important people, the honor of being included in this posh social group. To be invited is a feather in the cap of all social climbers and, perhaps more importantly, those people who consider themselves as socially lowly but who will now regard you as their hero for inviting them. They will inadvertently place you high on the social ladder, just for inviting them to this "exclusive" function.

Of course, they may reciprocate and invite you to their child's wedding down the road. This is the third reason you invite members of your committees: precisely so that they *will* reciprocate. If they do, you have one of two responses. Use response one, especially if the committee member is not, never has been, and never will be a mover and shaker in your community. You give your regrets, cordially stating that were it not for a pressing conference abroad, you couldn't be kept away (thereby reinforcing their idea that *you are actually important*). With response two, you attend the wedding but maintain an air of gracious superiority so that it will be clear that *you* are the important person with whom others wish to schmooze. Use the wedding as a time to drop your credentials gently to strangers. There are, after all, people you probably do not know who may be interested in joining your efforts to accomplish important things, *only if you make them sound vital and appealing*. Never attend any social function just to have fun. You must always view these functions as opportunities to spread news of your "important" work.

Now back to the committee meeting. What do you do with your daughter's engagement news? You must use this opportunity to broadcast it because it will create the illusion that you are actually friends with the committee members and that they would care about your personal life. You must use this all-important rule: *Ignore the aim of the meeting if you have something more pressing to say.*

In fact, say anything that gives these women the impression that you care about them (without actually befriending them). It is useful in making them feel as though you are friends and endears you to them. This goodwill is worth the few minutes it will take from your important meeting agenda.

Summary

In lieu of a quiz, I will provide you with the most important points from chapter12:

- Never divide your personal life from your public life.
- If you find you have too many responsibilities, call more lieutenants and volunteers.
- Never step down as chair.
- Pretend your committee members are your friends.

13. Never Really Let Go of the Reins

There may be times when your tenure is up, but you are not ready to step down as leader. Actually, if you are using correct leadership skills, you may never feel ready to step down. If this feeling has already swept over you, then congratulations are in order! That means you are well on your way to never having to do pedestrian work again!

If it is possible to pressure the organization to revise their bylaws so that you can stay in as chairperson, that is the ideal tack. You must do this quietly and gently, for if word gets out that you tried to change the bylaws to sneak in another term for yourself, and you fail in this endeavor, you may look like someone who does not know how to take turns or bow out gracefully. That said, you must do whatever it takes to keep your position elevated.

Never go gently into that good night by assimilating easily into the ranks of an organization once you have been its leader.

The trick about changing bylaws may not work in committees where the chair is elected (and you have just lost the election) or rotating (and everyone must get a turn). In either of those cases, it is far better to find a new committee than it is to be seen as a nameless face in a crowd of tireless little worker bees. Elected chair positions are better to avoid in the first place since elections are often popularity contests based on whether or not your constituency actually likes you, and—remember!—being liked as a real person is not your goal. Rotating chairs are fine to be a part of but then once you are no longer chair, try hard not to disappear into the rank and file.

It is better to desert the committee altogether than to lower yourself to the status of mere worker. If after deserting, anyone asks why you are absent from the committee, you must have a superior-sounding reason that keeps you away, and you must state the reason with pain in your voice so that everyone believes you would much rather be helping the committee you love. Having a bigger, better committee works well. Or you may resort to having to undergo medical tests for an unnamed but scary-sounding condition.

Let us assume that the office of chair in a particular committee was not an elected position, and the bylaws are firm and unalterable.

You must step down. Ah, but that is no excuse for fading into the background. Yours is a rising destiny, and just because you are no longer leader does not mean your organization is entitled to forget about your leadership.

You accomplish this in several ways. First, when your tenure is nearly through, you start making plans to hold a massive farewell party. You must not call it that or even hint that you would stoop to anything that essentially marks your failure to stay on. What you do is far more subtle. You casually mention to your board that in order to express your appreciation to them for their wonderful service to the organization, you would love to host a luncheon *in their honor* at your home. You send out save-the-date cards a few weeks in advance of the event and then formal invitations two weeks before the luncheon to ensure that everyone will be there.

Second, you assign a member of your board to order a few bouquets of flowers or potted plants for the people on your committee who have been unfailing in their work ethic. The act of delegating this duty to a board member firmly plants the idea that this luncheon would be the perfect time to honor you as well. She will, without a doubt, order flowers for you, but she will keep it a surprise. Then, without telling you, she will also call all the other members of the committee, and they will cook up some fabulous surprise gift to honor you. They may even collect money to have a plaque made to grace the outside the library (going back to our earlier example), and for generations, children will know their middle school library by your name. You may have to mention plaques in some obscure way at some point beforehand to get them to come up with this particular idea, but all it would take would be something such as "It is a pity that this little library doesn't have a plaque on it to dignify it. I wonder how expensive a little plaque would be?" You must not be obvious that the plaque should bear your name, or that would be a sure way to sour your committee on wanting that recognition for you.

Remember the best way to earn your status is to manipulate others into thinking they are doing this for you—that it is their idea.

Third, at the luncheon, you will give a heartfelt speech about what your committee has accomplished during your tenure. You will have gathered statistics so that not only will you enumerate every tiny goal, but you will also prove the success that your committee has had in furthering the overarching cause of your organization. Do not be afraid to draw comparisons to the organization prior to your tenure, but do it under the guise of applauding your committee's efforts, not in order to congratulate yourself (although your committee will mentally congratulate you if you do this correctly and that is exactly what you wish to have happen).

Then make a little speech about each member of your committee and mention something special each one did to further the cause of the organization. If there are members who did almost nothing, speak about them anyway but focus on their personal charm or some other characteristic that made them fun to "work" with. Then present the flowers to the select few who worked the hardest or had positions of most importance, being careful not to slight anyone who would expect flowers.

Fourth, make certain you have prepared an acceptance speech for the "surprise" that you know the committee will give you. When you accept it, you must feign surprise, you must appear humble (a pause while you sniff and wipe your eyes is a clever trick), and you must again credit the committee for all their hard work. If you have not assigned a committee member to order flowers thereby planting the idea of gifts and speeches, do not show any disappointment if a gift or speech for you is not forthcoming. *You can only count on something if you have prepared your committee to do it.* Showing disappointment will only make your committee feel they have failed you and will accomplish nothing in your favor.

Fifth, when the luncheon is nearly over, whether they have honored you in some way or not, make sure that you mention how much you will miss them in your new position as leader of that committee. Long before step one, long before the day when you know you will have to step down as chair, you must have found another post, even if you have had to manufacture it, much as you did this one. *You must not end this luncheon without something in hand to announce.* These women must have the impression that you are on to bigger and better missions. Do not be surprised if some of your committee members eagerly approach you to help with your new committee. Accept everyone who approaches you even if she has been difficult to work with, because the bigger your committee, the more societal recognition you will claim.

After this feel-good day is over, do not think your work is over. In order to stay in the game, you must plan a logical way in which you can still act as leader of your old committee in some capacity. Never mind that you have a new committee to run. *A good leader learns how to juggle more than one commitment by delegating more.* Allow some time to pass, say a year or two. It can't be so long that your community has forgotten your leadership, but it cannot be so short that the new leader resents you for apparently trying to grab the chair away from her. You create some anniversary that deserves extra attention. For instance, the 150th anniversary of girls' entrance into public school or the one hundredth anniversary of the first library west of the Mississippi or the twenty-fifth anniversary of Podunk Middle School. It must be something that tangentially has something to do with your former committee's mission, and it must be deserving enough of an entire celebration.

This next step is critical. Do not speak to the new chairperson about your idea. You must go to the head of the school, church, or community. The big guy, remember? From chapter 2. Do not pitch your idea unless you have researched it thoroughly because there must appear to be some merit for this celebration. And then to the big guy, you will say, "To make this anniversary significant, wouldn't it be a nice touch to have all the past chairs work together on it?" You will show him/her how each of the past chairs would work together as cochairs by taking one little area of responsibility from the chair. You won't *exactly* be the chair, but this trick will put you in the spotlight again as a leader. Being seen as a coleader is almost as good for your purposes as being seen as *the* leader. And it has the added bonus of reminding the big guy of who you are.

Summary

Again, no quiz! You are the luckiest woman on earth. I hope you don't drift into a lazy calm. You know I expect you to know the chapters without quizzes just as well. Here are the all-important notes from chapter 13:

- Try to re-up as chair.
- When stepping down is a must, plan a farewell party with flowers for you.
- Have an acceptance speech that expresses gratitude and announces your new position.
- Go to the big guy in a few years and organize a reunion chair opportunity with yourself as leader.

SECTION 2
Important Personal Skills for the Socially Aspirational

14. One Face Fits All

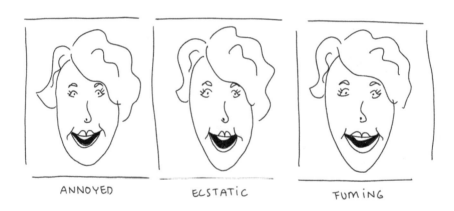

ANNOYED   ECSTATIC   FUMING

In some areas of the world, wearing your heart on your sleeve is not only acceptable but also encouraged. Women and men from Kosovo wail openly when they are sad, even in front of strangers. Italians and the French display wild gestures and hot tempers, respectively. People from the Philippines often wear an exaggerated frown when they are trying to impress you with how poor their circumstances. And the Dutch are notorious for their bluntness, for saying exactly what is on their mind no matter how rude it may sound to the American ear.

No matter what cultural idiosyncrasies you carry with you, if you wish to be a well-regarded leader, respected as the quintessential chairperson, revered as the most popular person you know, it is time to set aside all negative emotions.

You may feel them, but you may never again display them.

There are many reasons for this. The first is that, frankly, confidants cannot be trusted. What may seem to you like a simple annoyance with Ms. X, in the hands of the wrong person, may become fuel for tomorrow's gossip. Even if your confidant is your best friend. Even if you tell her in confidence. Even if you make her promise not to tell. In the leadership business—your business—one reason why you will be chosen for the head of committees over other candidates is because you will never bring any drama to your leadership. Let it be said of you that *you never speak ill of anyone* so that no one will fear to work with you, which, in practical terms, means no one will vote against you.

Along these same lines, the second reason you must not show any negative emotions is this: jealousies often abound. Of course, there will be those jealous of you. You are grooming yourself to be a high-profile, powerful woman who seems to be able to make anything happen. You will know people in high places (or at least you will give that impression). Importance radiates from you. See yourself as a local celebrity. As such, you cannot afford to give lesser individuals any kindling to put on your potential funeral fire.

Third (and my personal favorite), *you are not interested in real relationships with real people.*

They will only get in your way. Real friendships require give and take. Real friends expect that if they complain about something or someone, you will reciprocate. If you do not, they will feel as though you consider yourself above them. It is best not to complicate your overall goal by having real friends. Oh, you may indulge in the occasional out-of-town friend, but do not confuse her as a confidant in this era of the internet. Your only possible confidant is a spouse who you have trained well to be loyal and intensely private about your personal feelings, unless he is not the type to be close-lipped. If not, you may have to keep negative feelings and thoughts from him or her as well.

This means that no matter how Mrs. X rankles you with her continuous less-than-intelligent suggestions in your committee meetings, you must beam at her and thank her for her words, making a brief comment about her wisdom each time. If you cannot bear to do this with complete sincerity or if her comments are so inane that you believe referring to her comments as wise will make you look foolish, then you must simply thank her sincerely for her contribution and say something like "All ideas are welcome." It is a good idea to practice in front of a mirror until you achieve a genuine thankful look. Remember, your face cannot betray your heart or mind by giving the impression she has said anything less than brilliant or at least worthwhile.

Your job is only to keep everyone on your good side. You do that by keeping your personal negative feelings completely hidden.

The same applies to your personal positive feelings as well. No matter how much you genuinely like someone and wish to become her bosom friend, you simply cannot afford to curry any personal friendships where you indulge in sharing your true feelings. To do so puts you in a vulnerable position. Oh, you may have the odd date where you go to lunch or the movies with someone, but for two reasons, it is best not to ever go alone with one person.

First, if you find yourself alone, it may tempt you to let down your guard and speak candidly about someone else, which is bad for reasons we have already discussed. Second, it may give that person the impression that she is more important to you than others are, and she may grow to expect that your close friendship will earn her a prominent position in your committee. This is dangerous because when you are filling positions, you must fill them with people who will be the most advantageous to you, not those you may actually like better. Then if you fail to appoint your "friend," she might very well become your enemy.

You cannot afford to have enemies. Therefore, you cannot afford to have real friends either. If this is an upsetting piece of news, then you must evaluate how badly you want popularity, soldier.

Summary

Here are the most important points to remember if you remember nothing else from chapter 14:

- You may never show negative emotions.
- You may only use your spouse as confidant.
- You have no friends, not *really.* (I mean you have no *real* friends. I didn't mean that I was kidding about that.)

15. High Praise, Indeed

As we discussed in the previous chapter and elsewhere in the book, you must learn how to praise others for even their most absurd comments. The tricky part is that your praise cannot sound disingenuous, forced, or rote, even when you really want to cock your head and say, "Really? You think *that* is a good idea?" So get a pencil and a pad of paper and list several compliments you can have at the ready. Here are a few to get you started:

"I appreciate that you always contribute to our discussion."

"You are so full of ideas."

"It sounds as though you have thought long and hard about this issue."

"Thank you for kicking off our brainstorming session."

"I can always count on you to give a heartfelt opinion."

None of these is a real compliment in that you never pass judgment on whether the ideas are any good. Oh, come on. We've all done it. Think back to the time when your best friend gave birth to an ugly baby. You had to think of something to say that sounded genuine. You probably said something like "He's so sweet. I can see your husband in him." See? You gave the impression that you complimented the baby, but on close examination, you didn't compliment, nor did you lie.

So give the impression that you have given a compliment.

Due to the mere fact that you say anything with a friendly voice, it will probably come across as complimentary. Beware though. This can go terribly awry if by your pseudo-complimenting you actually encourage her to make more stupid comments. If this happens, and she truly tests your patience, simply stop the discussion and say (very sweetly) that you are sorry, but you have forgotten to lay out the rules of the meeting. The rules are that no one may give more than three comments per meeting to give everyone an opportunity to contribute. Generally, this will do it. Having said that, sometimes this opinionated soul will fail to take your rule seriously, and she will offer more comments. During her first sentence, interrupt her firmly but very kindly and remind her of the rules. Then offer to hear her comment off-line after the meeting is over. Usually, she will forget, but if she lingers to talk with you, that is a situation you can control more easily.

Quiz

I am sorry, but I am sensing that you are skimming my refined wisdom without internalizing it. Must I begin testing again? Take this short quiz to prove you were paying attention. Answer true or false.

   a)   It is not necessary to compliment every time.
   b)   Your compliments should be sincere.
   c)   Nip oversharing in the bud.

   Answers.

   a)   *False*
   b)   *False* (They only must *appear* sincere.)
   c)   *True*

(I will admit that b is a tricky one. If you recall, I said that your compliments should *sound* sincere, but they do not have to be *actual* compliments. After all, no one really has a good idea except you. If one were to be honest, you are the only one who deserves compliments, but do your best.)

16. Noteworthy

Another manner of dishing out praise is to send thank-you notes. With the advent of email, Facebook, texting, and other electronic media, handwritten thank-you notes are nearly *passé*. Certainly, they harken back to a more formal time when sending a thank-you note after a dinner appointment was an expected social courtesy. With today's casualness, a handwritten thank-you note from someone is truly a treasure.

Imagine how well received such a note would be if written by the lofty head of the committee (you) and sent to each peon (member of the committee). Just by deciding to send a thank-you note, you are elevating yourself to a level above the common man. And rather than send out a thank-you note willy-nilly (like every time someone makes a comment in a meeting), keep this practice special by sending the note only at the end of a big event or the end of your tenure.

Depending on what you say in your note, you may further boost your popularity simply by writing one. This is your chance to shine through. Don't just write any hokum that comes to mind. Whatever you do, do not do as the impatient high-school grad does either and create the same one-size-fits-all message for all graduation gift donors.

Since handwritten notes are a rarity in general, recipients may actually compare your notes to each other in the course of them bragging that they received such a treasure.

The notes you compose must be unique, clever, and use as many adjectives as possible.

You must never leave white space on the card. Write until you fill the card but not so much that you do not have room to pen your name with great flourish. These notes must sound as if you purchased them from Hallmark with just as much freshness, gushiness, flowery language, and finesse. In fact, it is best to actually purchase some greeting cards and tailor the text to your given situation rather than draft something unbefitting a committee chair.

Also, do not be afraid to exaggerate as long as it boosts your reputation as a generous committee chair and contains precisely one ounce of truth. For instance, let us suppose that the sum total of one of your member's contributions was to slap a pan of box-mix brownies on the table at a few committee meetings without placing them on a serving dish or providing napkins or plates. During her tenure in your committee, she neither made comments nor executed assigned tasks. In short, hers was a sorry contribution to your overall vision. You would say something such as, "Thank you for your extraordinary thoughtfulness in bringing your scrumptious delectables to our committee meetings. Thanks to your brownies, we felt energized, refreshed, and capable of executing all our book faire details with exactness and purpose. We have carried out a program vital to our school community, and I will truly miss working with this committee."

Do you see how about you never actually said *anything* about her capabilities? Yet you never let her feel as though her role was unimportant. Your note went far beyond merely thanking this member for brownies. Your note will give her the impression that without her treats, the committee simply could not have fulfilled their tasks. Her offering was more than adequate. Nay, it was essential to the success of that book faire. She will put your note in a keepsake box or frame it. At the very least, she will view you as someone who appreciates her. You have just added one more recruit to your I-am-the-most-popular-person-I-know camp.

In time, you might excel in the art of saying nothing with flourish, which will undoubtedly be confused with good writing by those who don't know what good writing looks like. Expect that everyone you know will rush to call upon you to write articles for school newspapers, magazines, op-ed pieces, church bulletins, executive reports, and more. People who hate writing these articles will remember your notes and will only remember that your notes completely bowled them over with your flowery-fluff style of writing. They will be unable to think of anyone better to pen their articles. Mere mortals are helpless against the power of too many adjectives, especially when grouped in threes. Rather than see through your silly and obvious attempt to flatter, they will fawn over your writing talents and beg you to compose their pieces.

Do not disappoint!

If it comes to it, you must burn the midnight oil to churn out this drivel because by so doing, your name will be further circulated, and your sphere of popularity will continue to widen.

Quiz

Yes, I am forced once again to quiz you, given the complete lack of attention you gave to last the chapter. It's okay. I'm not angry. (At least you will never be able to tell I am angry since I have perfected the role of a popular woman who does not indulge in such negative behavior.) Now do not disappoint me. I hope you do better than the last quiz. Please answer true or false.

a) Your notes are so valuable the recipient may frame them.
b) Your notes must never sound as cliché as a Hallmark card.
c) Your notes should reflect your great ability of writing well.

d) You should write thank-you notes often so that everyone you know will have one.

Answers.

a) *True*
b) *False*
c) *False*
d) *False*

(Remember, my little students, these notes only need to pass as good writing. In fact, no self-respecting English major would ever be caught dead writing the flowery nonsense that will become your specialty.)

17. The Artful Use of Sound Bites

Along with learning how to write differently, you must learn how to speak differently than you ever have before. You may chat with friends and acquaintances as you always have, but your style must change the minute you are in front of a group. You may think this requires you to think on your feet. Not at all. You just need to plan ahead. This takes several steps.

The first change you must make is the same change you made to your writing style. All the tips you just learned about using an inordinate number of adjectives apply when you are speaking as well. Put something together that you might read in a card, some non-rhyming verse, preferably with a group of three ideas, i.e., a soundbite. Think of everything you say as a possible quote one of your minions will want to steal and use.

Second, you must carefully consider your audience. If most of the people in attendance are peer leaders, you must take several minutes—in fact, nearly your entire time allotted—to stroke these peers for their phenomenal accomplishments. This is doubly important if these leaders are actually *more* accomplished than you are.

"Wait!" you say. "How can this make me look better than they?"

You are right. This is counterintuitive. Focusing attention on the triumphs of others may open the door to comparison, and there is a danger that your endeavors may look pale. But that is a risk you must take because what you are actually doing is firmly rooting yourself into *their* group. If there were any question about whether you belonged to this level of notoriety, pointing out their achievements in public makes you seem not only magnanimous but also—more importantly—*aware* of all that is going on in your community. You have identified yourself in *their* minds as a mover and shaker, someone who they would go to for community problem-solving.

If most of your audience is subordinate—that is to say, made up of people destined to be *on* committees but never to *lead* them—you must still take several moments to stroke them for their successes. If they are paltry, there is even more reason to trumpet them in public, even if all you do is point to their attempts. Those who are limited in their abilities will not be accustomed to such public praise, and *they will adore you for it.* Those who have tried hard, but perhaps not truly succeeded, will be so grateful to you for noticing their efforts that with this one act you will win their loyalty forever.

Third, you must thank those who have helped you achieve your goals. Again, stroke them. Make them appear invaluable to you but in such a way that the audience is clear that they were *your* lieutenants. Never state things like "I could never have done this without Mary." You never want to give the impression that you are *incapable* of moving mountains by yourself. Instead, you say, "Mary worked tirelessly to help me pull this off."

Always bring the attention back to you as the one in charge.

It is a subtle difference, but one that will subconsciously affirm you as an extraordinary leader. People will forget Mary in time and only remember that *you* performed this herculean task nearly on your own.

Fourth, point out what you and your committee have done in some detail so that there is no question what valuable service you have given to the community. Here is where you throw in testimonials. You should have gathered a quote or two from strangers who have gushed over what you have done. Actually, they don't truly have to be strangers, and they don't even have to be genuine. You could even just author a line or two before the presentation. Reading these "quotes" off a paper will legitimize them, and no one will question their authenticity.

It will appear as though great hordes of people are flocking to thank you for all you have done.

You will seem both praiseworthy and in tune with what the public needs if they have thus clamored to you to praise your efforts.

Fifth (are you still with me? I know. It's a lot), anticipate that you will be asked to speak, even if no one has mentioned this possibility. (This is a good general rule anyway. Prepare something for any occasion or gathering. I mean, you are nearly a *celebrity.* Expect that people will ask you to speak extemporaneously.) Prepare a few words of wisdom. Memorize a kernel of knowledge from some famous sage.

There is nothing so impressive or indicative of a leader as one who can readily spout great wisdom.

So plan ahead. It doesn't have to be your wisdom. Have something of value to say in addition to what you generate from your own mental resources.

Sixth, end your short comments with your statement of gratitude. Express thanks that the community has placed their trust in you for so great an undertaking. *Here is where you again brag about the magnitude of what you have done.* Never let it sound even remotely as though you are bragging though, even if what you did was to build the empire state building. You must always turn it back to the community and state how grateful you are that they entrusted you to undertake this monumental task.

Since you appear humble and grateful, no one will blink an eye when you say that this is the most important work the community has ever completed. Then leave it at that. You do not have to mention what a superb job *you* did at the helm of the committee. Now *that* would be bragging. *Your audience will get it loud and clear without you ever having to say it.* And you will appear humble while you are at it. Win-win. (See the quiz comments below for one more sneaky pointer about being humble.)

Seventh and last, you must do all this in true presentation style. Adopt a showman's pose and style of speech that makes it seem as though you were born to stand in front of an audience. That means you should practice in front of a mirror to check your appearance and posture. You should appear erect but not haughty, poised but at ease, well-groomed but not overly adorned. Your manner of speech should be warm but not familiar, devoid of ums and uhs, direct but not hard. Your speaking cadence should be slower than conversational speech to give you more time to think of your next phrase without any stammering. Review the speeches of any politician, especially presidential candidates. Notice how slowly they speak and how often they pause. Pausing not only gives emphasis to what they are saying, but if one is speaking extemporaneously, it buys one time to think about the next statement without having to resort to stammering or filling the gaps with ums.

Also, notice how politicians often adopt a more-polished manner of speech than they use in normal conversation. Your presentational speaking should be more formal in word choice and enunciation than your normal speech. We expected it of leaders. Audience members do not want to hear what the homemaker down the street has to say (even if that is who you really are). They want to hear what a leader has to say.

Sound like one.

Quiz

I know. It must be boring to take yet another quiz, but look at it as a learning opportunity. I'm really not checking up on you. Please answer true or false.

    a) The more paltry the contribution, the more important it is to recognize it.

    b) Admitting that you could not have accomplished a task without someone else makes you look humble and is a good idea.

    c) It is perfectly acceptable to generate your own testimonials to read in public.

    d) Expressing gratitude for the opportunity for what you have accomplished makes you look humble and is a good idea.

Answers:

    a) *True*
    b) *False, false, false!*
    c) *True*
    d) *True*

(Oh, little one! Did you truly miss the difference between b and d? Admitting that you could not have performed a task without someone else only smacks of weakness. Expressing gratitude is another matter entirely and does not usually appear as a weakness. And never ever, ever bow your head and cry when you express your gratitude. I mean, that *would* be appearing weak. Oh, and what a nice segue into chapter 18. Here we go!)

18. Emotions Are Greatly Overrated

Some might call it being superficial. I call it putting on a positive face no matter what the circumstance. If you truly want to be popular, this skill is key.

You must learn how to disguise all negative emotions.

You will hide all your disappointments, your guilt, and your anger. "Impossible," you say. "I am only human." Never fear. It is not as difficult as it sounds, and I, again, have compiled a handy-dandy checklist to guide you. If you adhere to it, you will become as fake, insincere, and wooden as every popular leader is, or as we expect them to be. You will deftly handle Mrs. X, whether she is jealous (see chapter 13), offended, or has failed to honor her commitments to your organization, all without offending her and (more importantly) while *maintaining your serene exterior.* Follow these steps to neutralize Ms. X.

First, you must contain the situation. Do this if she has let you know she has a problem, if you hear through the grapevine that she has a problem, if you sense that she is no longer a solid ally, or of course, if *you* have a problem with *her.* Ask Mrs. X for a time when the two of you can sit down and have a little chat.

Do not call attention to there being a problem because she might not wish to own it. Do not schedule your chat directly following a meeting or event in case someone is lingering and may overhear. You must aim for a completely private setting. Do not use a public place in case she is of the sort to cause a scene. Your name cannot be associated with such a scenario. Suggest your home. Her home is an alternative, but you will not be able to control the environment as easily, and you do not want her to feel as though she has the home-court advantage. Keep her less comfortable than she would like to be so that she will be less likely to behave as intensely as she may wish to.

Second, you need to neutralize her negative feelings. The first step in doing this is by telling her how much you personally value her friendship. (You must call it that, even though your relationship will never be that close.) Tell her what a huge contribution she is making to your organization and how much you and the others value her comments, insights, talents, work ethic, humor, etc. Fill in the blanks with as many things as you think legitimately fit her or that you think *she may think* fit her. (Did you follow that?) Stroke her ego as genuinely as you can.

After you have complimented her, she will feel less likely to go into attack mode. She may still have the same complaints, but she will probably deliver a watered-down version because you have taken some of the wind out of her sails with your "genuine" ego stroking. This step also works if you are the one with the negative feelings since it is difficult to compliment someone and feel negative at the same time. (That does *not* mean you lose sight of how you need to correct her, though.)

If she has a complaint against you, now is when you allow her the floor. No matter what she states, you must accept it and apologize profusely. You do not admit error or take blame, but you must state as humbly as you can that you are so sorry she was offended and that if there is anything you can do to fix the problem, you will heartily do so. You must smile and use the most soothing tones possible. Then you thank her for bringing this to your attention and compliment her on her honest and forthright manner. Tell her that you value knowing faults about yourself so that you can fix them. (Mind you, you won't really have to change anything about yourself. Heaven forbid! But you must sincerely promise Mrs. X that you will.)

Finally, thank her for being willing to sit down with you and work out your little differences in this adult manner. It will help if at this point you can muster a few tears in your eyes and a tremble in your voice so that she feels she has made an impression on you. She will probably want to hug you or squeeze your hands at this point, and you must respond in kind. Leave her with tears in her own eyes and intense gratitude in her beasty heart that someone in your position has condescended to talk with her and have a "real" connection with her.

If you have something negative to say to Mrs. X, you follow the same steps, except that after you stroke her ego, instead of giving her the floor, you ask her if she has any complaints about the organization that she would like to bring to your attention. Do not ask her if she has any complaints about *you*. You don't want to put ideas in her head. Give her the opportunity to voice any concerns, even though she most likely will not have anything to say. If she does, thank her for bringing it to your attention, yada, yada, yada.

Once you have gone through the preliminaries, gently but firmly launch into your disappointment of her performance. Do not spare her by underplaying how she has failed. Do it with a smile on your face, even if you are seething inside. Simply state what you expected of her and ask her for the reasons she did not follow through as asked. State that you relied on her and that she has personally let you down. Maintain your soothing tones and smile.

She might make excuses. You will expect that. With each one, you simply say, "You must always feel that you can come to me with any problem. We can fix most things as long as we know in advance. I need to know that in the future, I can trust you to either honor your commitments or let me know in advance if you cannot." You ask her to recommit to you that she will do this.

You may say that this looks suspiciously like what true friends should do with each other. Yes, it does smack of true adult behavior but with one important twist. *You never allow these confrontations to draw you closer to Mrs. X.* Nor do you actually alter your behavior to appease her no matter what you promise. You are not truly investing in this person as a friend. You just need to do whatever it takes to get her to cooperate within your grand scheme of world dominance, I mean, popularity.

The beauty of this approach is that you always appear to take the moral high ground. You never raise your voice or become defensive. You do not ever betray your true negative feelings about Mrs. X. You do not try to solve the problem by talking to other people about her. Instead, you find or manufacture qualities about her that make her feel as though she is invaluable to you and your organization, you promise the moon about what changes you will make to satisfy her, you throw in a couple of tears, and—voila—she becomes your groupie for life!

Quiz

Take this short quiz to reinforce the wonderful insights I have given you. Answer true or false.

a)   Admitting that you have done wrong is the sign of a great person.
b)   Listening to Mrs. X's complaints directly after a meeting allows you to nip it in the bud and is your best course of action.
c)   If you have a complaint against a member of your committee, and your anger is warranted, then you must reprimand with anger.
d)   Your popularity is the first step to world dominance.

Answers:

a)   *False*
b)   *False*
c)   *False*
d)   *True* (I mean, I sincerely hope so.)

(Admitting that you have made an error may be the sign of a great person, but I do not advise that for anyone seeking popularity. I will admit that the first question was just a little misleading since it may be true in the Judeo-Christian context. Remember that this is a quiz for what I am advocating, not what is *actually* true.)

19. You Are Not the Champion of the Underprivileged

There are some people in the world who will never be popular. That is just one of the sad facts of life. Perhaps these people lack ambition. They might be content enough in their little sphere of nonimportance. We need not discuss these people since they will most likely never ask anything of you or help you in your quest.

Having set that group aside, let us look at another group of unpopulars. These people wish to be popular or well liked—notice that I differentiated between those two states—but have inconveniently dull personalities, have no particular talents or abilities, or are downright unlikeable. What should you do about them? Should you offer them some help? Perhaps you feel you should do more than pity them. Perhaps as the magnanimous popular self-important person you are, you may think that it behooves you to help these unfortunates, help them to rise up and grab the few crumbs of popularity they might gain by association with you.

Stop right there.

Do not go down that ridiculous path. There is no room on the path to popularity for more than one, and *that one is you.*

Think about it this way: You have now spent a great deal of time, effort, and stratagem to hone your popularity. You may feel it is invincible. You may feel that your status is so firmly in place that nothing could knock you from your virtual throne. However, you must think of your popularity as a fleeting thing that will escape without your vigilance. It is as delicate as an old dandelion on a breezy day in spite of your current enviable situation.

You must never take your popularity for granted! You must never assume that it will remain in place without proper care. And one thing: Proper care means careful attention to your associations.

Not even the most popular people can afford tainting their reputations. Just look throughout history to see examples of popular monarchs who fell out of favor with their subjects because they associated with undesirables. And because they lost the favor of their people, insurrection ensued, and they eventually lost their crowns.

(Okay, maybe that never happened. I can't actually think of a single case right now when it did happen. It would make my job of convincing you much easier if I could. Never mind. If it didn't happen, it should have happened because this is a true principle.)

Do me a favor and imagine a scenario where you bring an unpopular social pariah onto one of your committees, and because of her presence, others begin rethinking the efficacy of your committee. (How can ABC committee accomplish anything with Ms. H on it? She has never done anything productive in her life!) Further, this practice could become a slippery slope. First Ms. H is welcomed on your committee, then Mrs. J believes that she can follow Ms. H's example, and before you know it, every undesirable is jumping on the bandwagon, and you have a complete entourage of incompetent social pariahs.

Just like that, you have earned the titles chair of the unfortunate, queen of the creeps, our lady of the social outcasts! By extension, everyone begins to question your abilities as a leader! Can you take that risk just so that someone you don't really care about might possibly maybe become slightly more popular than she was before you helped her? She cannot possibly rise to your level anyway, so why bother? Let her live her little dull life in peace.

It is really the kind thing to do.

Quiz

Fine. I am checking up on you to see if you are paying attention. Take this short quiz for your own good. Please answer true or false.

a) You can always afford to help others become popular.
b) You have the right to excuse social pariahs from your committee.
c) Popularity is a delicate thing.
d) Social pariahs eat people.

Answers:

a)   *Never!*
b)   *True by implication*
c)   *True*
d)   *Maybe true*

(We don't know all the reasons why some people are unpopular. Maybe they are not just dull. That last statement [d] might be true. Just one more reason to be wary of them.)

20. Nepotism Is Your Best Friend

Now after all this advice about not having friendships, I am going to state something shocking. What do you do if you have some *actual* friends in your life? Do they have a role to play in your quest for popularity? Or since they can no longer act as your confidants, is it time to call the friendship quits?

No.

I know, I know. I said that you could not afford to have real friends, but getting rid of the real friends would be problematic. Never fear. You may keep a few of them. They, too, can help you.

There will always be chances to appoint people or recommend people to positions for which you are either not well suited (i.e., the chair of an all-Icelandic choir when that is not your heritage) or are unavailable (i.e., the head of a committee in a sister city that would pose too much of a traveling burden).

Here is where nepotism becomes your best friend. (*Get it?*) Who made the rule that once you are in charge, you can't ask your friends to help? Or that you are not allowed to use your own children as models? Or that you can't ask your spouse to be the keynote speaker? Whoever made those stupid rules simply did not want to become popular as badly as you do.

The first rule you abide by once you become the head of a committee is that if you are not able to fulfill a role, look no further than your friends, children, or relatives. Slot them into that coveted position. You must make it happen.

Why should you not?

Doing this accomplishes two goals: One, you will have more influence over them than you would over a stranger, so it is conceivable that you could get them to do your bidding more easily. This is important if the role is a speaker at a function you are organizing, chair of a collaborating committee, or any other role where you will need their cooperation. Two, if the person you appoint or recommend is related to you, your name would be out in public twice as often because twice as many people with your surname will be achieving notable things.

Their efforts will reflect back on you.

I hope that you are in the position of appointing the friend/ relative directly, and there is no one with veto power. You can slip your "pawn" into position before anyone figures out that you have just doubled your sphere of influence. If you must recommend the pawn to someone else who holds the power, remember this one trick. When making the pitch, you must distance yourself from the friend/ relative.

This becomes a bit of an issue if your pawn is a relative with whom you share a last name, especially an uncommon one. It doesn't have to be fatal to your recommendation, however. You would be surprised how many people will not catch the connection as long as you act as though no connection exists. Here is how you do that.

> You will say, "I understand you are looking for a keynote speaker for the movers and shakers symposium."
>
> Ms. Z will say, "Why, yes. We are having a hard time finding someone. Do you have a suggestion?"
>
> You will say, "Actually, I recently attended a meeting of the best millennial entrepreneurs, and I heard one fabulous and engaging speaker who I think we would be lucky to have. He kept us entertained for nearly an hour explaining how his company, Solar Plexus, is developing a new method of solar heating that eliminates the need for those ugly solar panels on your roof."
>
> Ms. Z will say, "Solar panels?"
>
> You will say, "I know what you are thinking. Isn't that so relevant to our community's ideology? It will appeal to all our environmental friends. That was just what I was thinking too. Great minds think alike! The way Valentino Latour explained the technology was just fascinating!"

> Ms. Z will say, "Do you think we could get him for our September symposium?"
>
> You will say, "I happen to know he is free and that he would waive his fee for us."
>
> Ms. Z will say, "That is more than I had hoped for! We could have a dessert and cheese reception with the money we save!"

Notice how you slipped in your son's name without focusing on it. You focused instead on what he could do for Ms. Z. In addition, you did not mention that he is related to you. Never say, "My son would be a great keynote speaker. He spoke at the best millennial entrepreneurs meeting and was so good." That is very bad.

First, no one wants to book a speaker who is just an acquaintance's son. It is true that even Bill Gates is somebody's son, but if being related to *you* is not something your son would put on his résumé, then don't say it. Focus only on his qualifications. Second, no one is going to remember the best millennial entrepreneurs part because they will stop hearing you after you say, "My son." And third, no one is going to believe anyone's mother to be objective in her assessment of her son's performance. They will assume he stinks as a speaker.

Now your exchange with Ms. Z might not go as smoothly as the example above. Ms. Z might stop you the minute you say your son's name and say, "Latour? Is he any relation?" You deftly move past her question like this.

> You will say, "I can't believe you haven't heard of Valentino Latour. He's not just a who's who in solar panels. His skill set applies to so many industries that he is a popular speaker for a broad range of businesses. I just hope he isn't fully booked in September."
>
> Ms. Z will say, "Do you think we could get him for our September symposium?"

You will say, "I can give you his contact information. Mention my name, and he may waive his fee."

Ms. Z will say, "That is more than I had hoped for! We could have a dessert-and-cheese reception with the money we save!"

You are so wily. I am very proud of you right now.

Do you see how you, again, use your son's full name as though he is not related to you, as though he is a completely independent person? And then you sneak that little worry into the conversation about his availability. This has the effect of putting your son in the realm of desirable people in demand and throws Ms. Z into panic mode over the fear that she might not be able to secure his services. She suddenly becomes desperate to get him! The last thing you did was to tell her to mention your name. That makes it seem as though you and he are both important people in your own right, and your names are almost commodities in themselves. It also further distances Taylor Latour from you as merely your son.

So nepot away. (If that isn't a verb, it sure should be. How else can we describe this very necessary action?) Push your children, your spouse, and your close friends into positions of power and influence. Then learn to become a puppet master. After all, of what use is it to place them into positions if you can't control them?

Quiz

Here is another quiz I am forcing you to take because I care that you internalize this stuff. It hurts me more than it hurts you. Answer true or false.

a) The only way you can be popular is if you have an important son.
b) It is in bad taste to put your family members into positions of importance.
c) *Nepot* should be a verb.

Answers.

a)   *False* (although it can't hurt)
b)   *So Very False*
c)   *True*

(Well done. I think you are getting the hang of this popularity thing.)

SECTION 3
Exploit Home and Family, or the True Reason for Motherhood

21. What's in a Name? Could a Rose by Any Other Name Actually Stink?

I do not pass judgment on whether you should or should not have children or whether you should or should not get married. For the purposes of this book, it also does not matter what gender your spouse is or whether you are cis female, trans female, or any other gender identity. Any of the above scenarios have their advantages and disadvantages with respect to your popularity. I will assume for purposes of this guide, however, that you have chosen to have children since many of the women who are advancing a social career in the volunteer sector are mothers. So let's accept that you decide to have a few children. How can these children benefit from your social climbing?

The first thing to consider is the naming of the child. Some people do not subscribe to the philosophy that a name makes the man (or woman). Parents in this camp might give their children names that they like because they are pretty or popular.

Beware! A popular name does not necessarily beget popularity.

In fact, the opposite is probably true.

Naming your daughter Brittney because every little girl on your street is named Brittney (and because not all those parents can be wrong, right?) is foolhardy. Your poor daughter will feel forever compelled to explain to her classmates and acquaintances which of all the many Brittneys she is. She will be required to give her surname every time she introduces herself, especially over the phone, and she will often need to explain that she is the tall blond Brittney Smith that sits in the back of Mrs. Cordova's fourth period history class. Yes, the one with blue eyes. Yes, the Brittney on the volleyball team. No, not the one dating Dexter B.

Do you see how cumbersome a name like Brittney is? *Do not burden your child with this weary task.* Give her a name that stands out all on its own. (Note. Brittney is otherwise a perfectly wonderful name for all you who think I'm hating on the name Brittney.)

Let us back up for just a second and say if you are married to or descended from someone who has a famous name, it might not matter what first name you give your child. After all, even the name Brittney Gates or Brittney Obama will carry weight in most circles because of the famous surnames. Let us say, however, that you have no famous name, and in fact, you have a very common surname like Smith. Almost any first name paired with Smith runs the risk of being ordinary simply because the name Smith is so common.

The knee-jerk reaction might be to go overboard and give your child a name *no other human being has ever had. Parallelogram* or *Gonorrhea* are names that certainly would beef up the surname of Smith. Just. Don't. I. Beg. You. The name must have grace and dignity too.

Likewise, you might want to name your child something that harkens back to one of your own accomplishments. Something like *Canada* points to the fact that you were the first woman to ever trek across the expanse of Canada from the Pacific to the Atlantic. Not bad. It could work. But don't go too far. A name such as *Harvardette* would certainly be unique and remind others that you indeed *did* graduate from Harvard. (Or that you at least attended. Okay, fine! Your sister applied there.) I have to say that I might rather *not* be popular than to saddle my unsuspecting child with such an obviously made-up and hokey name.

Grace and dignity, my friend.

So search in the archives of existing names and come up with something that will stand out and eliminate the chance that your child will linger in anonymity. Alliteration never hurts either. For instance, September Smith stands out, is not hokey, and takes advantage of alliteration to boot. It might even be the month that you met

Barbara Streisand. You could spin that to your advantage every time you explain why you chose that name.

Now as to the name making the man, or woman: Because you have given a name that is rather high profile, your child will grow toward high profile-ness. More than likely. At the very least, it will be hard for that child to succumb to anonymity. That is all we are aiming for at this moment.

A name that will stand on its own and maybe even drag your child up with it.

Quiz

I am sure you will be able to conquer this quiz. By this time, I trust that you are actually paying attention and maybe even taking notes. It is *your* popularity that is at stake, after all. I am already popular. Answer true or false.

a) Naming your firstborn Harvardette is a clever way of letting people know that you (almost) went to a certain prestigious school.

b) If you have a common last name like Smith, you'd might as well give up trying to become popular.

c) No one should ever name her child Brittney, unless it is a boy.

d) If you have named your child the most popular name of the decade, he can kiss his popularity chances (and yours) goodbye.

Answers.

a) *So false*

b) *False (You can't help what your parents or husband did to you. You will only have to try harder.)*

c) *False (Brittney is a perfectly good name, even for a girl.)*

d) *False (There are many other ways to become popular.)*

(Well done, little grasshopper.)

22. There Were Never More Special Children than Yours

The minute my children were laid in my arms after their births, I knew they were special, amazing, and destined for greatness. I very much doubt that I am alone in these beliefs. Many people think *my* children are special, amazing, and destined for greatness.

Of course, what I meant was that many people think *their own children* are special, but their belief does not make it true. I really don't believe that all of them, if pressed, would actually say that their children are *wunderkinder*, that they will cure cancer, develop the next techy device, or become president of the United States. They are content to have their children be special *to them*.

But if you want to become popular, you should consider grooming your children for greatness from their first breaths because their accomplishments will reflect favorably on you. I hope that you have followed my advice in the previous chapter and branded them with an unforgettable name. However, do not stop there. From the time they are old enough to understand—scratch that. *Before* they are even old enough to understand, teach them that they are a cut above everyone else.

This means that at school, your children should believe they are better than everyone else, including their teachers. That attitude could cause disciplinary problems. That is why you must be careful to combine your indoctrination of specialness with (a) a healthy dose of respect for authority figures and with (b) the need to be kind. Do not go overboard in teaching those two attributes, however.

Remember the ABC cartoon *Milton the Monster* which aired in the '60s? His creator, Professor Montgomery Weirdo, accidentally used too much Tincture of Tenderness when forming Milton; and rather than becoming a scary Frankenstein-like monster, Milton was tender to a fault.

You do not want to groom someone who is so kind that they are completely deferential to their teachers or who are so compassionate that they lose their competitive edge rather than hurt a classmate's feelings. You want strong fearless children who will make the most of their potential, not children who bow to others' wishes.

Besides, kindness is overrated. It is the movers and shakers like you who actually change the world, not the Mother Teresas. (Don't tell anyone I told you that. I suppose she was a great woman. *Whatever!* But was she popular? I hardly think so. Otherwise, she wouldn't have been out there in India, saving orphans on her own. And before you get your panties in a twist, of course, I was joking. No one should ever say anything bad about that magnificent woman whether she was popular or not. Shame on you for laughing at my poor joke.)

So focus on all the amazing accomplishments that your children are expected to perform in their lifetimes. Stroke them daily with your vision of who they are and what marvelous things they are destined to do. Help them to see that they are uniquely smart, creative, talented, and privileged enough to do the impossible, *tailored to their specific talents and abilities.* That last caution is important. If a particular child is poor at mathematics, telling him that he will become the world's next Albert Einstein might only prepare him for a lifetime of defeat, and you will eventually find yourself with a forty-five-year-old loser living in your basement because he is convinced he can't win at life, only at video games.

Also, be careful only to stroke and encourage without demanding excellence, or like the children of many stage mothers, you may end up with either (a) children who succeed but hate you or (b) children who rebel early and choose a less demanding path.

None of those kinds of children is best suited to assist you in your quest for popularity, so resist the urge to beat them, even verbally.

There is a third sort of achieving child. You might end up with overachievers who still love you but who are more focused on furthering their aims than yours. While these children will already be useful to you for bragging rights, do not allow them for one minute to focus entirely on their own accomplishments. Drill into them the idea that a family who succeeds together loves each other more (or any other such nonsense that helps them to see that helping you is part of their success). They must see that they can be beneficial to your path to success. It is important that you raise children who can also do your bidding when summoned.

I mean, yours is a herculean task. Why should your children expect you to accomplish it on your own?

Quiz

Yet another quiz to prove that you are actually taking in my wisdom. Answer true or false.

    a)   Mother Teresa was kind to orphans, and we should all aspire to be like her.

    b)   If your children do not excel at anything, they will never be special, and it is your duty to remind them of that often.

    c)   Forty-five-year-old children living in one's basement make poor comrades in one's quest for popularity.

    d)   Mark Zuckerberg hates his mother because she demanded excellence of him.

Answers:

    a)   *False (I mean, of course, in real life, this answer should be true; but it is absolutely false if you are trying to achieve the kind of popularity we are talking about.)*

    b)   *False (Your children were born special simply because they are your children, and you will tell them often that they are. Also, compare them to other less-impressive children to reinforce this obvious fact.)*

    c)   *True (Do not raise children who cannot be an advantage to you!)*

    d)   *False (I hope.)*

23. Your Children Are Spectacular, or At Least Not Spectacles

What happens, you ask, if you have one child who just cannot rise to your expectations? Perhaps this child is akin to Milton the Monster who, in spite of all your efforts, is just too kind to have any room for ambition. Or your child is quite average without any outstanding qualities but has siblings that excel. On the other hand, perhaps your unfortunate child lacks adequate intelligence to attend college or qualify for any job beyond a drive-through cashier.

What then?

Hopefully, you have more than one child, and with some deftness, you can focus attention away from the inadequate child and onto the more capable ones. You do not do this to the point of embarrassment for the ill-starred child. When listing your children's accomplishments, you merely state the notable ones without attaching a child's name to them so that the listener believes you have listed the endeavors of each child when, in fact, you have only listed the many undertakings of one very busy child. That way, it appears to the listener that all your children are changing the world and that, therefore, *you are the head of the world's most enviable family.*

The second tactic for dealing with a non-achieving child is to find something—anything—that sounds better than a run-of-the-mill, ordinary service job. For instance, using our above example, let us say that based on her aptitude, she is destined for a career at McDonald's or Taco Bell. (Not that I have anything against either of those fine establishments, one of which employed me for two weeks in high school. High school students in my day and neighborhood did not have many other options, so stop judging me. High school students in my day and neighborhood did not have many other options, so stop judging me.)

Here is where you move into high gear and find something of which your child is capable that sounds impressive to an outsider and that, ideally, is not a job where said outsider can confirm that your child is working at a questionable position. This may take a bit of money and will certainly be a time-consuming operation.

You must find a job, even that of a drive-through cashier, which is abroad in some exotic place. A cashier in Sapporo, Japan, for example, will impress acquaintances, and they will infer that your daughter they thought they knew well must have possessed hidden qualities that made her a solid candidate for such an exotic position. I mean, you don't see their average child earning a position in Japan. They will think, *Maybe she wasn't so average after all.* They will conclude that you have the world's most enviable family.

Alternatively, you could elect to keep her stateside but find a nonpaying internship that sounds impressive. For instance, perhaps you are able to arrange a greeter position at your spouse's office. This is a position that requires very little competence but carries the weight of your spouse's firm, or if he doesn't work anywhere impressive, you will have to make up something impressive. In conversations with others, you say, "Yes, my daughter, September, is doing a fabulous sociology internship studying the greeting rituals of North American male elites."

You don't bother to say that she is unpaid, that her position is useless, or that the internship will not result in any substantive dissertation. Nor do you state the obvious, which is that this so-called internship is just a fancy way of saying she hangs around the mall all day boy-watching. Your only job is to make her meager accomplishment (or complete lack thereof) into something extraordinary. That also goes for the cashier job in Japan. Even a crappy job in an exotic place is still a crappy job *until you spin it.*

Once you have spouted this near fiction about your child, you must also be prepared to spout details, if pressed. That is because other parents who aspire for good jobs for their children will want to get in on the action of this spectacular sociology internship. You've already given it some credibility by stating the whole title of the internship. Now you have to manufacture an organization, location, hiring director, and supervisor. Details! It's all in the details.

Again, what is your mantra? *You should not lie outright, just spin the truth correctly.* The best option for a false organization is your spouse's company, which is, of course, not a fiction and which *just happens* to need a sociology study. Never mind that he works as a plumber or landscaper. To disguise the name of the company from the prying Ms. X, you can use the unfamiliar formal name or the initials of the company for which he works. Never mind, too, that no one in the history of either plumbing or landscaping has ever commissioned a sociology study. Ignore all that. Sociology is so vague you can apply it to any field. And apply you will.

Here is how your conversation will go.

> Ms. X will say, "A sociology study? That is remarkable. Who is she working for?"
>
> You will say, "Oh, JSP [a.k.a. Joseph and Sons Plumbing]. They are hoping to understand the male mentality." (Read. They thought this study would increase their customer base. Not that there is really a study or that this study would or would not increase their customer base.)
>
> Ms. X will say, "Is it a paid position? I'd like my Donna to try an internship like that. Who can I contact?"
>
> You will say, "It is not a paid position, but it is such an honor for her to be a part of this study that a salary didn't matter."
>
> Ms. X will say, "So who can I contact?"
>
> You will say, "Honestly, I know this is the last year they are conducting the study, but I'm sure if you speak to the high school counselor, they can help you find a similar study."

See how you never really give any details about the study? And you completely skirt the issue of a contact person. If you are pressed, for instance, about what type of company JSP is and what the study will do for them, you have two good choices. Either feign ignorance (not hard to do in this context) or you could continue pushing back with vague factoids such as *they want to increase their customer base* or *they are concerned that their product only appeals to women.* Keeping it vague, having a few good details, and then dismissing it altogether by stating that this is the last year, should keep the Mrs. Xs of this world at bay.

Oh, finally, if you have children who actually excel, brag away. However, never sound superior when you do it. No one likes a braggart. I've said that before (see chapter 2) because it's true. You must say something like, "Oh, your son is going back East for school? I will tell my son, Sven, to help him become acclimated into Yale's physics department." When she corrects you, stating that he is only going to Podunk State, you cordially say that you have heard good things about that school. Your acquaintance will remember, not just that your son is studying physics at Yale but that he must be a thoroughly helpful guy with a gracious mother.

Such an enviable family!

Quiz

Yes, another quiz to keep you on your toes. No falling asleep when your popularity is on the line, after all! Answer true or false.

- a) Your children must attend prestigious colleges in order to boost your popularity.
- b) A crappy job in Japan is as good as a crappy job down the street.
- c) Nonpaid internships can sound wonderfully elite if you spin them correctly.
- d) Children who do amazing things bring honor to your name and help your popularity.

Answers.

- a) *False* (although it can't hurt)
- b) *False, false, false!*
- c) *True*
- d) *Duh*

(I cannot believe you almost missed d! Why do most women have children anyway if not to help their volunteerism career? If you did not answer d correctly, do not pass go. Do not collect two hundred dollars. As punishment, reread this chapter again before continuing.)

24. Contests Confirm What You Already Know

By now, you and I know that our children really are the best, smartest, most spectacular children on earth. (How could they not be when we, the best, smartest, most spectacular women on earth, have spawned them?) It never hurts to establish your opinion as fact, however, because if it becomes fact, then you can wield it as evidence of your family's obvious superiority and that will boost your popularity greatly.

How does one do that, my friend? Watch and learn.

There are a number of ways to establish your children as the best, but let us start with the easiest. You start by insisting that your child develop a skill such as playing the violin. You will have to pay tutors or private instructors to make sure your child excels at this chosen field. Do not stop there, however. It is not sufficient for your child merely to hone a talent. You make the most of it by doing three things. (1) You volunteer your child to perform everywhere and anywhere. (2) You make a complete scrapbook of all the performances and competitions. (3) You enter your child in every possible contest.

Let's flesh these ideas out a bit, shall we?

First, let's look at volunteer performances. These are important because they will have the double effect of turning your child into a minor celebrity, and they will get him/her used to performing in public for an appreciative crowd, which will bolster his/her ego. Most parents will consider the once-a-year middle school orchestra concert where their child is fourth chair second violinist to be sufficient for displaying their child's talent. Not so! These annual performances do little to serve your popularity. Think, woman! Think!

If you attend a church, speak to the pastor and convince him/ her that your child's playing would greatly add to the mood of the Sunday devotional. This may be the norm for your church. If so, sign up your child to perform several times a year. If this is not the norm for your church, you may have to do some convincing by researching biblical passages where music was used to a great effect (think David calming Saul with his playing or Jericho's walls falling down at the sound of the trumpets). Help your pastor consider it his/her ecclesiastical duty to provide angelic violin music at least for the Sunday prelude. But don't stop with your church.

If there is a PTA meeting, offer to have your child play for the ten minutes prior to beginning in order to calm the crowd. If you hear of a grocery store or a twenty-four-hour fitness center or any other business opening a new store, talk to the organizers in advance and offer free entertainment in the form of your child prodigy. If there are readings at your local bookstore, offer your child to play beforehand to set the mood. When organizing all this, emphasize that your child is a world-class performer who is willing to waive his/her fee in order to benefit local enterprises. Saying this will motivate people to take advantage of your child's largess, regardless of your child's actual abilities. Before you know it, your child will have a full schedule of volunteer performances.

Now comes the real work. You must document each and every performance as if it has taken place in Carnegie Hall. Take pictures (plural) of your child performing and pictures (at least one) with your child standing with the organizers. If there are programs, make certain your child's name appears in the program and keep a copy of it. If there are no programs, it doesn't hurt to design one with your child's name and short bio in it. Jot down any comments made from audience members after the performances to use as testimonials; these comments can be from such unbiased persons as your spouse or mother if other such audience comments are shockingly lacking. Scour the local newspapers for any write-ups of these events, especially if they allude to your child's performance and even more especially if they mention your child by name. Armed with all these items, compile a complete scrapbook detailing all the many times your child has appeared in public. If you keep a scrapbook of your child's vacations, school papers, and other interests, do *not* combine the two. This is solely to be a scrapbook of why your child is approaching celebrity status.

"Why do I need such a thing?" you ask. "Who is ever going to see this?"

Humph. Must I teach you everything?

Everyone who is anyone will see this work of distilled brilliance, a.k.a. the mighty scrapbook. Here is where the contests come in. You begin entering your child into local contests, competitions, draw-ings, and pageants. I've been in a beauty pageant before. I observed that, despite its name, beauty is one of the least-important factors in winning a beauty contest. The most important thing is one's presentation.

I was in a beauty pageant when I was young. I lost big time (as in I didn't even place) because I naively thought that my looks and piano skills would easily carry me to win. The woman who actually won had no real talent other than arranging a mini fashion show. That is, a number of her friends walked across the stage in clothes she claimed to have designed and sewed. What she did have was what I lacked: She had drawings of her designs and photos of her outfits compiled in a massive scrapbook dating back ten years. The judges were overwhelmed at her *supposed* talent even though—let's be hon-est—she didn't actually sew or design or perform anything *in front* of the audience as the rest of us performance artists did. She only had reports of what she *allegedly* had done in the past. But apparently, that was enough. She became queen. She was beautiful, but then most of us were.

So enter your child in contests, pageants, and competitions, but then do not leave the results up to the judges. Bring your fabulous scrapbook. Present it on a lovely tablecloth with a piece of violin music that your child has supposedly composed along with any med-als and awards. (If your child has earned no awards or medals at this point, generate some yourself. It is easy to manufacture awards on your color printer at home. Medals and trophies will cost a little money, but may be worth the cost to give the impression that your child is a winner.)

Include a dish of truffles in a crystal bowl, and the judges will linger longer to peruse your child's accomplishments. They are only human. Once it comes to the judging of the actual competition or con-test, the whole presentation will sway them. They will flip through the scrapbook longer than they would have because of your elegant treats. Your child will most likely win, regardless of talent (or lack thereof).

Of course, this win might be very nice for your child with self-esteem building and all that, but do not lose sight of your true aim. This win is a feather in *your* cap.

Now you have someone of note who you can use as evidence that your family is the best!

Quiz

Given your near failure on the last quiz, I must insist that you try your best on this one. Are you sure you are ready for this? Would you like to give this last chapter one more look-see before attempting this quiz? Here goes, then. Answer true or false.

a) Beauty contests are not always won by those who are the prettiest and most talented.
b) Documenting your child's burgeoning talent is almost more important than the development of said talent.
c) It does not hurt to manufacture awards, ribbons, and medals to prove your child's accomplishments.
d) Requiring your child to perform often will scar her/him for life.

Answers.

a) *True (I am the talented, most beautiful walking proof of that.)*
b) *True*
c) *True*
d) *False (But would it matter if it were true?)*

25. What? Your Child Could Not Have Possibly!

Some mothers parent by overindulgence. Others are wonderful disciplinarians. Others load their children with so many chores that they don't ever get into mischief and form wonderful work ethics besides. All those styles have their virtues. What is the correct style of parenting for the woman seeking popularity, though? Let's examine each.

You certainly don't want overindulged children (even though I am sure any children of yours are so special and spectacular they *deserve* to be overindulged.) Think about it though. Usually, children who are overindulged grow into tiny dictators, demanding that Mommy satisfy all their wants and needs. Their universe revolves around them. They have never learned the importance of thinking of others, namely you. You have no use for such creatures because (a) they will use up your valuable popularity-making hours and render you exhausted; (b) they will not be compliant, resulting in children who refuse to do your bidding; and (c) they may even become vindictive when you do not pay them enough attention and blab your motives to their friends and neighbors. Who needs those kinds of children? No. Resist the urge to emotionally stroke these radiant, clever, perfect children you have born. Of course, this will not stop you from bragging on them to others, but do not make the mistake of letting your children know that they are deserving of all your time and attention. No child is worth your time and attention if you truly wish to become popular.

From the moment they enter this world, begin grooming them to do your bidding. You may have to feed them. Clothe them. That sort of thing. You should even tell them that you love them so that they will become loyal to you. But don't gush over them to the point where they expect you will always be there for them. Keep them guessing so they feel they have to earn your love. That will make them into more pliable minions. This may be tricky to accomplish while also letting them know they are special. (See the previous three chapters.) I will admit this is tricky. My advice is to keep your goal in mind and remember the *purpose* of your children. They are on this earth to further your popularity career, *not to actually be spectacular people on their own.* They can focus on that when they have their own children.

Should you discipline them? Yes, otherwise they will feel that they can do as they wish. You have no use for children who have minds of their own, who feel they are in control, or who do not realize the proper purpose of their existence. Do it fairly, however. You don't want children who may one day mutiny and cause your whole popularity empire to come crashing down. Or worse.

What about the chore issue? While chores are important if only to free you to spend more time on your popularity, your goal is not to mold children who become adults with character. I mean, if they grow up and actually have some character, I suppose that's fine. Two birds with one stone.

Nevertheless, your focus is *you* not *them.* Your goal is to create children who will have just enough work ethic to succeed in a skill or craft that elicits notice from the public (thereby adding feathers to your cap) while having not so much work ethic that they are driven to hone their own skills to the point that they are loath to take time away from said honing to assist you. It's a fine balancing act that will require some practice on your part. Keep your overarching goal in mind, and you will succeed.

What happens if these finely oiled machines that you have created misbehave? What if you have accidentally created children who have over-internalized their unique specialness? What if the children are arrogant and believe that others are lesser beings? Worse yet, what if your children misbehave in public so that other adults take notice? What then?

Take this scenario. Your child behaves well, at least around adults. She says appropriate things to teachers, is very polite to parents, and never dreams of making a scene. Think Eddie Haskell of the famed *Leave It to Beaver* show. (If you are too young to have missed this dated classic, it is worth a search, if only to view a perfect social devil.) On the flip side, this child is devilish to one of her peers. For no apparent reason other than maleficence, your darling begins to whisper to the girl next to her in third period that she is ugly and fat. She does this constantly and so stealthily that no one else hears these insults. To the girl's face, your child is charming and kind, so when the girl complains to the teacher or her peers, no one believes her.

Finally, in desperation, the child turns to her parents who do believe her. They are decent people and call you for a meeting to discuss the problem. In your home, they tell you the extent of your child's shenanigans. They tell you the effect it is having on their daughter. They cry. They plead with you to make it stop. How do you handle this embarrassment? First, never bring your child into the meeting. Your child might make things worse by admitting to the indiscretion and apologizing. Now you have an entire family who knows your child is less than perfect! No, resist the urge to bring your child into the picture.

Second, do not become embarrassed. You have no obligation to believe these people. Then offer your sincerest comfort to the parents. You use your most gentle tones while stating that no child should ever have to endure such treatment at the hands of a bully. You agree that this horrible situation must stop. You tell them that every child is precious and that you feel personally ill that this is happening to their child.

Then you stop.

Look the parents in the eyes and say, "But it cannot possibly be my daughter who is saying these things to your child. My daughter would never do such a thing."

You ask them how they know such awfulness is occurring. Has anyone else seen your daughter behave in this manner? Has your daughter been disciplined by the teacher, for instance? Before they answer, you quickly state that the teacher has never contacted you or hinted that your child was anything but a golden-haired student.

When they answer no—as you know they will—you provide evidence of your child's goodness. You tell them how your daughter volunteers as an assistant Girl Scout leader, how she is your neighborhood's favorite babysitter because she is so beloved of the children, and how she goes out of her way to compliment her teachers and friends. She even helps at the local women's shelter and food bank, for heaven's sake. Your daughter, you tell them, is absolutely incapable of what they are suggesting. It is counter to her very nature.

If they resist, offer more evidence and, again, offer your sympathies. You offer to get to the bottom of this by suggesting your daughter act as detective to find the real culprit. You applaud them for being champions of their daughter's rights. You tell them that you believe bullying is a vicious practice and indicative of poor parenting. You suggest that the real culprit is probably a child whose mother has a demanding job outside the home and does not have the bandwidth to carefully guide her child. You sympathize that both of your daughters have to be in the same classroom as children whose parents are simply not aware of what their children are doing. *You lay it on thick, baby.* Even if you suspect that your angel is the culprit, you must create enough doubt that they will want to believe another child is to blame.

The parents will leave believing their daughter might be in error as to who the bully is. Even if they still suspect your daughter is evil incarnate, they will leave believing that you are the most wonderfully understanding woman the world has ever known. They might even wonder how such an evil child—if it turns out the bully in question actually is your child, of which at this point they are uncertain—could possibly have come from such a gentle, caring, kind woman such as yourself. *You see?* You have deflected suspicion from your child and as a bonus, and these parents will come away with boundless admiration for you.

And what becomes of your darling? Why, nothing! You have seen *no real evidence* that your child has done anything wrong. Clearly, the victim is mistaken and her parents misguided. Besides, whoever this bully is, she is behaving discretely. (You allow yourself a moment where you internally congratulate this little bully—*whoever she is*—for employing such deft tactics! Not that you for a moment approve of the actual bullying. That would be wrong.)

Quiz

No quiz. (You have earned it.)

26. What Happens at Home Stays at Home

Your best-laid plans for creating the allusion of family perfection may at times become derailed within the confines of your home. No parent is *always* present when children have disagreements with each other. No adult contains his or her anger *all* the time (including yourself). No one can control all the unpleasant and would-be embarrassing things that your family may do at home. What does this mean for your plan to create the allusion of perfection? Because, everyone already believes that *you* are perfect and, by extension, that *your family* must be perfect. What can you possibly do to keep up that front when you know that quite the opposite is true?

This is, admittedly, a formidable task. This complex task is not one you can handle on your own. You must anticipate and silence all possible leaks from all possible sources. You must vigilantly monitor these possible mutinies. You can never relax or *assume* things are going smoothly. This is the scariest and most monumental task of them all, because there are so many factors to control, and you cannot be present all the time with all your children. You must simply indoctrinate your family to realize what is at stake and behave accordingly!

Your knee-jerk reaction might be (1) never to have children in the first place; (2) after giving birth, keep said kids home at all times; or (3) never allow friends to visit.

Let us just debunk those rash ideas one by one, shall we? First of all, you need those children for all the many, many reasons mentioned above. They are invaluable for getting you to your popularity goal. The more bodies are working on this effort, the more potential your popularity has of growing exponentially. It's simple math. So do not wish those children away.

The second reaction is bad for the same reason. If your children are not in the community doing great things or talking you up, you have missed opportunities. This popularity goal is too difficult to accomplish on your own. You need them. Moreover, you need them *out there*, where they can be influential.

Let friends come over. I see no problem with that either. We all know that children behave better when their friends are around. Why shouldn't they? They are getting what they want. There will be fewer fights (if any), more cooperation with you, and pleasantness abounding. The last thing your kids would want is to have their friends feel their home is a depressing or angst-filled place where their friends will never want to revisit. For sure, your kids behave their best when friends come over. Besides, those visitors will then go home and personally attest to your family's perfection.

It is a toughie to keep *all* family imperfections hidden but not impossible.

Here's how.

It requires beginning almost at birth subtly to coach those eager minds. You must tell them that they are not the best, most perfect children *in a vacuum*. That is, they are only the best most perfect children *because* they came from the best, most perfect family. This means that every time they succeed, you reference the family while praising the children. It sounds something like this. "Oh, Carlish, you played that violin piece so well. That is what Johnsons do!" or "Jakarama, of course you caught that impossible throw. You are a Johnson, after all." Once they understand that concept, they will be more apt to protect their magnificent family.

Do not stop there, however. You must remind them that tiny family infractions are just that. Tiny. As in not gossip worthy. And family matters. As in, just the family needs to know. You don't say it immediately after the great family blowup either. To do so makes it seem far more important in your children's minds than is warranted.

No, wait until the incident is well over, preferably at night, and then you will casually say, "That was a bit ugly today, wasn't it? Well, in families such as ours, one has to expect that geniuses will clash. It is to be expected. However, we do not need to advertise these clashes to others. They, of course, would not understand that is how it is in talented and clever families. Not everyone is so lucky, so they wouldn't understand."

Occasionally, tidbits of your family's imperfections might slip out. Do not see these as betrayals by your children when these stories come back to you. Best just to ignore those as untrue gossip. Laugh them off as if they are slightly funny jokes. *Giving them your attention only validates them.*

Quiz

No quiz. (Don't tell me that I have let you off the hook too easily. You are still gleaning the wisdom from each page, correct? Good girl.)

27. Intimate Dinner Parties Might Require Actual Friendships: Don't Be Tempted

It is always fun for a family to receive an invitation to eat in the home of another family. It warms the heart as a truly lovely gesture. It makes one feel a better connection to the community. It introduces children of different ages and spouses from different walks of life to one another. The result is that strong bonds of friendships often begin with such invitations.

All that sounds fine if you were to want real friendships.

Is that your goal? I ask for the hundredth time. Should you be extending invitations right and left? No. You can't be bothered with such antics and here's why.

First, inviting another family to your home implies that you want a level of closeness that, frankly, is a waste of your time. You do not truly wish to become friends with anyone. As we have read previously, friends are not necessary or even desirable to achieve popularity. You have no use for such a level of intimacy. So don't invest your time in something that might even take you further from your goal.

Second, what will you talk about with these invited trespassers? You will have to generate answers to personal questions, the type people assume they can ask when invited to another's home. The invitation itself brings a tacit understanding that the host is open to ramping up a closeness that will ultimately amount to a friendship. This will put you on the spot to divulge things about yourself that might give the impression you are *merely human*. You cannot keep the conversation on committees or lofty goals *in your home*. The setting invites familiarity.

No. Better just to keep them out.

It doesn't matter if another family has invited you to their home, and it is your turn to reciprocate. Ignore such silly conventions. And by the way, if you do accept an invitation to someone else's home, stick to comments about their home, their children's school activities, or their dog. Never ask about the hosts themselves, or they will assume a closeness you do not want, which might foster questions you do not want to answer. Keep yourself above such trivial pursuits.

Third, you do not have time for such nonsense. (Inability to schedule the dinner will also be your excuse if pressed for an invitation.) You were meant for greater stuff than mere domesticity. Those who you invite will expect a home-cooked meal that you have made with your own two hands. Once the invitees have seen you standing at your stove with your face all sweaty and your arms elbow deep in pasta sauce, you will forever be branded as the domestic one, the good cook, the sweaty gourmet! That is all well and good for some women who are seeking that kind of notoriety. However, these skills *in you* might cloud your guests' vision of you as the popular one, the head of committees, and the most important mover and shaker they know.

R-E-S-I-S-T.

Summary

I noticed your attention waning for a second. I will sum it up for you so that you don't have to reread the whole chapter.

1. Dinner parties invite friendship, so never go to them, if you can help it.
2. Just because some friendly gal invites your family over does not mean you must return the favor.
3. It is never good for others to see you sweat.

28. Throw Parties Often and for Any Darn Good Reason

Having said all that in the previous chapter, I will now apparently contradict myself and say you must invite people to your home often. I stand by what I said in my previous chapter. The difference is that if you extend any invitation whatsoever, it must be to as *many* people as your home can hold. A party setting removes you as the sole focus. Suddenly, you are the host of a large gathering of interesting people. Let them converse with and entertain each other. You will busy yourself with hosting, not bearing your soul to your guests. *Big, big difference.*

What does this do for your popularity? It is twofold, really. Over time, your home will become known as the party destination, the place where interesting people gather, the not-to-be-missed special event location. You will become known as the person who is so popular that when you throw a special event, others will go to ridiculous lengths not to miss it.

How does one achieve this status? The key is not in your decorations or the food. It is not dependent on your witty hosting banter. The key is that you will invent an interesting reason or theme. You will invite an excess of people so that you end up with a full house, and you will hold these events at least quarterly so that an expectation develops among your acquaintances.

I will break these down for you.

First, the interesting reason. Anyone can throw a baby or bridal shower. These are fun, but they are dependent on someone having a baby or getting married. Since you are not really close to anyone because so doing interferes with your quest for popularity, those someones may not choose you to host their big parties. You must, therefore, generate events on your own. You could use a holiday for an event, such as Easter. Then rather than holding your event on the actual day of the holiday (when families will probably be busy with their family traditions), you hold your event the day before and call it Easter Eve or some other made-up but clever name. That will ensure interest (Who has ever heard of Easter Eve? What's that?) and the greater likelihood that you will get a large turnout.

On the other hand, take a Christmas event. Rather than holding it on Christmas Eve when most families are busy with their own traditions, throw a Christmas Adam Party. (What is that? Adam was created before Eve, so "Christmas Adam" is the day before the day before Christmas.) Christmas Adam is realistically too close to Christmas for most people to want to accept, but you get the idea of how to parlay a holiday into an event *for you.*

During those months when we have a dearth of holidays, you will simply have to think of an event. Think of any hobbies that several of your friends share, such as dancing. You can hold a dance exhibit at your home where these friends can perform a short routine for each other. Alternatively, if you are about to kick off a new committee or accept a new position in a committee, throw a get-to-know-you luncheon to provide a social setting for committee members to become acquainted. Perhaps you know a local celebrity who can kick off a monthly lecture series in your home.

Any event will do. Except.

It must *never* be a Tupperware party or any other multilevel marketing scheme or forever after, your home will be associated with needing something from the guests, no matter how good the product may be. By the same token, your event cannot be a girls' night out watching *The Bachelor.* It is not interesting enough, and you do not want to be associated with meaningless activities. Leave those events to women who actually want to be friends with each other.

Once you have sent out clever invitations that outline the interesting reason for your event, call many of the invitees and ask them to bring food items. You cannot hold events often if you also provide the food. Doing that would force you to be known as the domestic one and put a strain on your budget as well. Plus the beauty of this arrangement is that once people commit to bringing food, it increases the chance that they will actually show up and feel a vested need in making the event a success. How many wins is that? I counted three wins in that arrangement.

Good on you.

29. Why Be Private when Publicity Works to Your Advantage?

This chapter is also known as one more thought about hosting events. In keeping with the idea of hosting interesting events in your home, things happening in your personal life are not off-limits. Let us suppose that you have a mishap and fall down the stairs, breaking your ankle. Your natural inclination is to rest in your bed and keep this embarrassment from others. But you do not do that. This is an opportunity for an event!

First, you make it known through your children, spouse, committee members, and neighbors that you have injured yourself. You should tell your children to tell everyone they know that you will not be able to attend their school concert/play/match because you are severely injured through no clumsiness on your part. Your spouse should similarly, but casually, drop hints to neighbors, coworkers, and golf partners that he must pick up fast food because you have severely injured yourself. (He should do it in such a way that it is not dramatic as in I-am-telling-you-this-in-passing-not-that-we-need-assistance kind of a way.) You then call various committee members under the guise of gathering information or assigning a task to them. You casually say that you would gladly do it, but you have been confined to your home under doctor's orders. You do not say this dramatically but as a matter of plain fact.

After this information has been allowed to circulate a few days, you send out invitations to a cast-signing luncheon. You must take advantage of your injury to rally your troops. Do not think for one minute that you will retain your popularity by laying on your sofa watching soap operas, even temporarily. You can follow the doctor's orders just as easily while being surrounded by women who want nothing more than to serve you in your time of need.

Do not appear needy, however. Tell them when they ask—and they will ask—that it is not necessary to bring in meals, watch your children, or clean your house. Either you will hire others to do those things or you will rely on a relative. Accepting help in your time of need makes you appear incapable, weak, a victim.

You tell them that you simply wish for their company and coming to your cast-signing party will serve that purpose.

Follow your event rule about assigning food and games. You might even assign someone to bring fancy markers or stickers with which to sign. Voilà! You have a party, and you didn't even have to think of a theme. Your body did that for you. Lucky you.

And remember to behave yourself at the event. Do not succumb to their requests for you to emote about how much it hurts, how clumsy you were, or anything else that gives away your personal feelings.

Keep it light, breezy, and matter-of-fact. You may state that you have a new piece of hardware in your ankle but only if that proves interesting because you just happen to know the woman who invented that particular screw. Or you may give details about the length of the operation if it is because you were delayed in pre-op by a scrub nurse who couldn't stop thanking you for all you had done for the community. You get the idea. Only supply details if they prove interesting, or further the impression that you are *somebody.*

Oh, and if before anyone arrives, you have to down a slightly larger dose of pain pills to do so, then bite the bullet and take them. Anything to create the illusion that you are fine, just a bit inconvenienced by your cast.

30. If Your Spouse Is Powerful, then So Are You!

Whether you have a career of your own or have focused on volunteer work, you might not be as well-known as your working spouse, especially if your spouse is a husband. Let's face it. Few women with children have as much time to pursue their celebrity as their husbands do. Let's say that you have a husband, and he is a mover and shaker in his field. If you have a husband who has done something notable, this becomes your accomplishment too. It is only fair. If your husband's field is medicine, and you simply have not been to medical school, that is a small matter to rectify. You must leverage his education and career to your advantage anyway.

This works best if you attended the same university as your husband when he was doing his doctorate. You can—without a lot of lying—say, "When we were at Yale together getting our PhDs." While it is true he was completing his dissertation while you were barely making it through your English Lit class or even doing very well academically but then failing to defend your dissertation the essence of your statement is that you were at Yale together. Others will think you were also completing a PhD in physics. No need to correct them. If they ask specifically if you have a doctorate in physics, you use the royal *we*. "Yes, we do." It cannot be a lie if the whole British royal family does it.

Another way to use the royal *we* is when employing a more-general tactic. Whenever you speak of his education or training, you say, "Yes, when we were in medical school." when you were never, never ever enrolled. What? You think that's wrong? Why, husbands do that all the time when talking about giving birth. They say, "We're having a baby! We're in labor!" And the worst, "We're pregnant!" None of those statements is remotely true or possible or even shared. If that were true, women would be able to "share" their pain, discomfort, bloating, weight gain, etc. But they can't. And yet, men get away with making those blatantly untrue statements all the time. *So can you.*

The other way to leverage your husband's education is to refer to him by his title. If he has a medical degree or even a PhD, a dentistry degree, or is a chiropractor, it is customary to refer to those persons as doctors. Even a law degree translates into the title Doctor in academic settings. If your husband falls into any of those categories, you must "accidentally" refer to him not by his first name but as The Doctor as if you are just referring to him the way everyone does. If someone calls you on it, just slightly roll your eyes and say something like, "Oh, he's funny that way. He likes me to call him that. He calls me that too." The little eye roll is designed to bring the other person into your confidence as if you are both chuckling at your silly marital idiosyncrasy and so they will not take it seriously. They may then ask point-blank if you are a doctor. You just smile and laughingly say, "Yes, didn't you know?" They will think you are making a joke (not telling a lie), and in the end, they will remember your husband is a doctor and maybe you are too.

If he's not a doctor but is very good at what he does, still use a title when referring to him. Call him The CEO or The Guru or The Whiz. Whatever fits. And don't forget the tiny eye roll as if you have no choice but to call him that if you want to keep your marriage alive.

Or if your husband is a public speaker, make sure he thanks you publicly with tears in his eyes, not for "being a good companion" (too vague) but for "giving him specific ideas," which he will then enumerate. This will require some coaching to make sure he gets it right. Or if he happens to be the president of the United States or any other public figure, and you are invited to speak because of whatever fancy job he has, make sure you pull a Rosalyn Carter now and then such as, "Well, the energy conservation plan that I, er, my husband, *we* developed is very important." I think we were confused at times who was running the country. Good for her.

There is a caveat to your husband being impressive. When titles don't apply, as long as you can parlay his job into something that sounds impressive, do so. You simply have to spin it in a way that makes it sound impressive. (That is spin doctoring 101, my friend.) Once you have done that, just use the other techniques for taking credit. For instance, if he inherited a mom-and-pop greengrocery long before you came along, you say, "It really wasn't anything until we got our hands on it." Take credit for every. Possible. Thing. He. Does.

31. Have Your Spouse Nominate You for Things

This section will be for those whose spouses are in a position of some power. Before you look at your high school janitor partner snoring in his barker lounger and dismiss this section altogether, let us look at your options. Remember this first and foremost with a nod to Nora Ephron: Every spouse is copy. (Okay, *that* didn't translate.) What I meant to say was that every spouse can do good for your cause. So maybe he has no sway as a janitor, but look at it this way: He is in a position to have his ear to the ground in the high school. Important things are posted on the walls such as plays, club meetings, dances, tests. Even if you have no high school student, you can take this information and volunteer to help. (Once you volunteer, then you form a committee, yada, yada, yada, and you are *in!*)

Let's say, however, that you had the forethought to marry someone who has brains and a bit of ambition. His current job reflects that. He is in a position to recommend you for things, and he should without prompting. He should know you by now. However, if he has a momentary lapse in the importance of who you are and what you can do, ask him about his company, brainstorm with him, and remind him that you are a competent person with abilities. Groom him to look for opportunity.

Is his office, where he is the head accountant, screaming for someone to organize a job shadow program with the local high school? You are just the person. Does he, as head deacon of your church, need someone to lead a youth choir? You can do that (even if you pretend). In his capacity as the head of a nonprofit, does he recognize that you could be the great motivational speaker his team needs? The point is, he must be ready to volunteer you whenever an idea surfaces at his company (if it does not need to be handled by an employee of the company.) He needs to be so well versed in getting you *in the door,* that if his company were to think bringing in a trained seal handler would get good publicity, your name should leap to his lips volunteering you for the task.

Never mind that you can't begin to do what he nominates you for. Either you will learn how to do it on the fly or, better, you will organize the committee that will orchestrate it to happen. You will simply get it done. Either way, your name will be all over it. Thank you, Hubby.

SECTION 4
Members-Only Club:
Keep Out the Riffraff

32. Form Exclusive Clubs that Meet Regularly

I apologize in advance to any of you who take offense at this chapter because you love your book club, and they let in everyone and their dog. Or at least everyone on the block. Boo-hoo is all I have to say to you. Give yourself a little slap for being such a sissy.

Gone are the days when you could join a club just for the fun of it. If that is the life you want for yourself, you'd might as well be a part of the Tupperware-selling club. Not that there is anything wrong with it, unless you would like to become the most popular woman you know, which you would. You know you would. Don't lie to me.

So look at every opportunity as the possibility for advancement. This includes your golf club, book club, stamp-collecting club, or mah-jongg club. It does not matter what the hobby. You can and must make it exclusive.

Here's how. First, you slyly speak with a few people who have accomplished something in their lives. You needn't bother with those uneducated nonproducers you know, regardless of how fun or sociable they appear. Stick to those who generate envy in others. It is fine if they are actually nice people with whom you would like to associate anyway, but never think of this trait as a prerequisite for an invitation to your book club group.

Once you have selected three or four people, set up monthly meetings that each have a different theme. If mah-jongg is the hobby you have chosen, you might have a south-of-the-border night where you play mah-jongg, but the decorations and food conjure up images of Mexico. The next month, which will have rotated to a different host, might be fifties-retro with food and decorations to match. Maybe a book club would work better than mah-jongg, but regardless, the point is to get each host to outdo each other so that each of you will not be able to resist speaking of it to others.

Because that is the whole point of the club, after all, to speak of it to others. This tool reinforces your elitism because you cannot create elitism without the have-nots looking in and yearning to join.

So you will just casually mention that you attended this fabulous party. Don't speak of it in a bragging or condescending way as if you are glad that your listener was not invited. No, do quite the opposite. You must speak of it in hushed tones as if you are so grateful that you had been invited, and you wish with all your heart that your listener could have been there too.

You never let on that you are the instigator of the club. In fact, when you are gathering your club members, you should never say that it was your idea. Allude to another member as the instigator, using a different club member each time. Or say that it was a mutual thing that just happened. That way, when others ask to join (and they certainly will), you can apologize that it is exclusive and out of your hands.

In tandem, you will talk to all the members of your club and discretely mention reasons why you should keep the membership numbers low. Mention the lack of space. Talk about how fulfilled you all are with just the members you have. Soon, it will feel like a violation should anyone ask to bring a new friend. If anyone does try to bring a new friend, emotionally shun the friend (while being polite to their face) and then speak to the member later about how it is not the intent of the group to bring just *anyone* in off the street. Help her to see that it is not a decision one member should be allowed to make on her own.

The main thing is to keep the club going forever. It could even be a dinner club where spouses and children attend too. That might make it unwieldy over time as participants add new children or in-laws, but this will also give plenty of opportunity for others than yourself to distribute the happenings of this very exclusive club. Yes, your listeners will agree that only someone like you would belong to such a club.

You must be very popular indeed!

33. Join an Already-Booming Club

There is no need to reinvent the wheel at every turn in your quest to become popular. That means you do not have to stay with the volunteer library helpers group, just because you had your start there. They have served their purpose. Now move on. You cannot afford to be emotionally attached or be loyal to a club or organization if there are greener pastures. In fact, only stay with them until you have been able to create a buzz around your name and your accomplishments with the library helpers. Then it's time to look for a more prestigious group.

We have already discussed how to form an exclusive club, but this option is better when there are simply no people with whom to form a club who are as exclusive as you would like them to be.

This should be a group with some prestige. It could be an alumni group for your alma mater. It could be a support group for entrepreneurs. It could be the Rotary Club or the Elks or any number of traditionally established clubs. The point is you must employ the same tactics with your listeners as you have previously with the club you formed (or would have formed if there were any notable people with which to form such a club). That is, talk up every event as though it were the social event of the year.

Remember the name and credentials of every speaker of note. Remember the quantity of money they collected and donated to the boys club. Note the fine clothing, particularly witty conversation, the menu, and the table gifts—anything to report back to your listener.

Watch her salivate for want of being there.

34. Apologize to Your Friends that They Can't Join

If this is not a traditional club with bylaws—let's say it is a neighborhood book club that has been going on for ten years—do all in your power to make it become exclusive. That is, once you join it, offer to host. Once you are the host, you can crank up the decorations, finger foods, and themed party favors. It won't take too long before others are following suit. What was once a nonchalant little group among friends has suddenly taken a Martha Stewart detour. This is when your bragging can begin in earnest.

Again, as in the instructions in the last chapters, you mustn't brag as though you are trying to make anyone jealous. You must brag as though your heart is breaking that your listener could not attend. "But when are these book group meetings?" she will plead. You will become evasive and tell her they don't follow a regular schedule, which is up to each host to determine.

"Oh, please!" she will cry. "Please tell me when the next one is coming. I'd love to join you. I will even read the book."

The first time she does that, you will nod and assure her that you will let her know. End the conversation right there, and don't even think about letting her know when the next meeting is. She must go for several months before you "remember" to bring up the book club again.

When you do, you must be effusive as always. You must brag while not appearing to brag. Use that special tenderness all loving parents know who must deny their child something that is not good for him but which he desperately wants. Using that voice, describe how witty the refreshments were, matching the fairytale theme of the book exactly. Tell how you made an exceptionally good point about the protagonist's ulterior motives. As an afterthought, outline what a beautiful shade of mauve the host used to drape the display table that held her fairy house collection.

Once again, your listener will remind you somewhat urgently that you had promised to invite her to the next gathering. At this point, you stop and place a motherly hand on her shoulder. "Oh, I am so very sorry, my dear," you say with tears in your eyes. "Did I not tell you that this was a closed group?"

She will stutter and remind you in a somewhat feeble way that you had promised to let her know about the next meeting. You must apologize and say that the club presidency had just determined to close the membership. You will say that because there were getting to be too many members, one host simply could not accommodate everyone who wished to join. You will shake your head woefully as though this was not your decision (which it was), that it was out of your hands (completely within your power to change), and something with which you would never agree (so very false). You will utter your parting statement, "I wish there were something I could do," and walk away.

The next time you launch into your bragging, do not be surprised if your listener looks on you with a slight betrayal in her eyes. She knows she has been duped. She must never know that you intended to dupe her, however. You never want to be in the business of collecting enemies.

The way you cure that problem is by offering to help her generate her own book club. You give her a few pointers such as what people she should invite, the maximum number to have, and the inclusion of a theme with decorations. (Do not give her very good information. Hold back on most of what makes your club magical.) Soon, she will have her own lesser nonexclusive group that she may never have the energy to sustain.

Even if her club doesn't flop, never give her the satisfaction when bragging about it. Of course, she will try to let everyone know that she is now the proud organizer of an elite club. You will simply smile and let her talk, resisting the urge to trump her. She will wait for jealousy to creep across your face. She will wait for you to ask for an invitation. You will simply sigh and state that it sounds like she has a nice little group going. "Good for you," you will say as if speaking to an ugly cousin who has just become engaged to be married. Give it the right mix of pity and happiness, and she will think she has really accomplished something.

Do not allow yourself an indulgent giggle as you walk away.

35. Praise Paltry Lesser Clubs when Possible

If you handle the above scenario in chapter 34 graciously enough, soon your competitor will realize you never ask for an invitation to join her club. If you keep up with *your bragging* long enough, however, she may become annoyed that you refuse her the opportunity to show you her group is just as good as yours. This will only work if you steadfastly refuse to give her any credit for her efforts in the form of jealous looks or entreaties to attend.

You must style your response in the way that people with old money treat the *nouveau riche*. It really is immaterial to them how much money the newly rich have because they know in their hearts that new money is never a substitute for old money with all its confidence and reach. Besides, the newly moneyed tend to display their wealth with gaudy excess. It is so beneath the old money guard.

So it is with you. Be confident that you have arrived. Your club is the true and only club anyone wants to join. Many inferior clubs will spring up in time. They will come and go. Hold on to your exclusive elite group confidently knowing that no one could possibly measure up.

There may come a time when your club competitor may ask you to join her club, not as a member but as a guest. This is merely a trick to get a rise out of you. She is desperate to show you that her club is better than your stupid club that would not give her admission.

If this happens, you must accept. Turning her down will only frustrate her and may cause her to nurse her petty disappointment into really animus.

When you arrive, smile cordially without really engaging. Stay composed the entire evening without emotion, no matter how fetching the decorations are. Be polite without being genuine as you give your book insights, meet her friends, or answer questions about your club. Say as little as possible so that your competitor has nothing for which to fault you.

At the end of the evening, thank her kindly and throw her a bone. "I can see you've tried so hard to make this nice little club. Congratulations. It must be so fulfilling to see these people appreciate what you've accomplished."

I mean, no need to go overboard on the praise. Give her just enough that she is lulled into believing that she has done a wonderful job all the while knowing that her club pales in comparison to yours. No need to do the comparison for her either. Her imagination will do that for her in spades. And your club will win every time through no fault of your own.

And don't forget your pity/happiness face as you say it.

SECTION 5
The Cheers Factor: Once Everyone Knows Your Name

36. Name-Dropping Is a Virtue

Let us suppose for just a moment that you have met someone famous. It could be a high school chum you have lost touch with, someone you haven't seen in twenty years. It could be the friend of a friend. It could be your sibling, your aunt, your neighbor, your college roommate. It doesn't matter who it is as long as (1) this person is recognizable and (2) you can credibly establish your connection to this noteworthy individual. "A credible connection?" you ask. What is that? Let me explain: Anyone who has skied or attended an event at Sundance, such as the famous film festival, could have seen Robert Redford. That chance sighting qualifies as something novel, but just seeing him doesn't get you anywhere. A sighting, as it were, does not establish *actual connection.* Your peers will think that you are lucky, like seeing the solar eclipse, but just seeing him does nothing for your social self-promotion.

However, if said Robert Redford happens to be married to your cousin's aunt three times removed on the in-law side of the family (a.k.a. no actual relation to you), then you have something. Then you can say, "I saw my cousin, Robert Redford, at the Sundance Film Festival." Suddenly, your peers will stand up and take notice. They will forever associate you with Robert Redford. You, the relative of one of the most famous Hollywood stars.

Watch for naysayers. They do not have your back. They will try to trip you up and get you to confess that you are making this all up. When that happens, do not back down. All you have to say is "Yes, he is my cousin on my mother's side. They are all Redfords." Don't deign to explain yourself. Who cares that he is not a blood relative, that his wife doesn't keep in touch with your cousin's family, that Robert Redford's wife has not studied her genealogy and has no idea who these cousins are or even that she may not currently be married to him. None of that matters. What matters is associating your name *credibly* with his.

And don't stop there. Once you have linked your name with his, bring up your connection occasionally. If you name-drop continuously, that just turns you into a celebrity wannabe. People can see through a feeble attempt to glorify yourself on the notoriety of another, and they will subtly roll their eyes whenever you mention Robert Redford. This will surely do damage to your self-promotion.

So what do you do instead?

You hint at the connection whenever possible. For instance, you say, "We are vacationing in Provo this year at the Redfords." The truth is that you are flying into Utah and will probably take in a community play at the Sundance Theater among other things. You will be on Robert Redford's property, you will be on vacation, and you are *relative enough.* Others will make the plausible inference that you will actually be spending time with Robert himself, all without actually speaking his full name.

37. Pretend to Be Uncomfortable with Celebrity

By now, you should have become fairly popular in your community. That is, if you have been studiously following my directions. And by popular, I mean that people hear your name and exclaim, "Oh, *her!*" And when they hear you are the head of a committee, they sign up because they know that committee will accomplish good things and that they might *become popular* by being a part of it. When you throw a party, people are thrilled to be invited because they know all the *popular* people will be there. If your child is getting married, they will want to come because *even more popular people*—like the mayor—might be there. Of course, it is within the realm of possibility that the mayor would be a close personal friend of yours. They will believe it is possible because they believe you are *someone to know*.

This is when public things start to happen for you. You will be asked to speak at a high school rally. Not because you have any connection to the high school but because you seem to be *someone from whom everyone wants to hear*. Not because you have anything substantive to say either but because you *seem* professional and important because you are popular and presentable. Moreover, you have the ability to make people feel good about themselves. (All lessons from previous chapters. Don't forget.)

If you are asked to speak at that rally, PTA meeting, presentation to the school board, political town hall, or anything else, you must always accept. And prepare your remarks assiduously so that you can have something of substance to say.

Before that, though, you must do the most important thing to bolster your popularity. You must pretend that you are slightly embarrassed at the invitation. We discussed in earlier chapters how if your committee honors you with a gift for a job well done, you must feign embarrassment. Remember? You do this even though you were the deft puppeteer who practically forced them to give you a present.

This situation is no different, although, by now, you know you deserve the honor; and you are definitely the *most qualified*. You must still feign discomfort at all the attention that is coming your way.

Why is this important? Because no one likes a smarty-pants. No one likes someone who is good at everything or who wins every time. "But this is *me* now," you say. "You have groomed me to be someone who is good at everything and who wins every time." Which is precisely why you have to feign embarrassment. If you show that it was the furthest thing from your mind to have been selected, people might actually believe that you are nice, kind, and the victim of your own success. Poor little you. People will almost feel sorry for you if you do it correctly.

You start by saying things like "You want *me* to address the League of Women Voters? What an honor. I was not even *aware* they had a chapter in our community." You say this with complete believability, even if you have been currying the favor of the president of said league for weeks.

The same holds true if you have nagged your spouse for months to ask you to be the speaker, choir director, rally organizer, or community liaison for the church for which he is pastor, or any organization for which position he has the power to appoint someone. Once he actually calls you, make sure he announces it in front of an audience because that will give you the chance to display your discomfort.

Perform the same little act if someone runs into you with someone you don't know. They will most likely introduce you with gushing pride as in "This is Susan McCambridge-Hool. Yes, *that* Susan McCambridge-Hool. The one I've told you so much about. *She* can do *anything!* She's *really* someone you should get to know. Aren't we *lucky* that we ran into you, Susan?"

You very calmly and sweetly say, "Oh, I'm so pleased to meet you, Anne, was it? You know your friend, Mary, here is such a hard worker. I could not have run all the fabulous committees I have presided over without Mary by my side."

Never mind that Mary hasn't really done anything at all on any committee.

Once you have finished bragging on Mary, she and Anne will virtually genuflect away from you, twittering all the way. Notice that you didn't counter what Anne was saying. You didn't deny that you *can* do everything because, of course, you can do everything. It is true. Instead, you have shifted the focus away from yourself and onto this poor heap of a woman.

The added bonus is the next time you run a committee, Anne will wet herself trying to get on it.

38. Brag about All the Work You Have Done but Disguise It as a Willing Sacrifice

It should be completely apparent to you by now that you are a bit of a celebrity. You are probably on several committees. Did I say *on?* Correction. You are probably *leading* several committees. You know whom you can call upon in the community to assist you. You know who will do all the work and leave you to the finer things such as, well, all the above tactics. And these tactics take time, as you have seen by now.

By this time, your phone will be ringing off the hook to chair this committee, speak at that function, or even give interviews for articles on how to lead others properly.

Then that call will come. The one that you knew would come one day. The call that asks if you will accept the *Nobel Peace Prize in Leading a Committee.*

There isn't such an award?

No one told me. Well, there should be. If there were, you would be the recipient—absolutely—for at least two years in a row.

Let us say that instead, a different, slightly lesser call comes from the Lion's Club, Churches International, or the Junior League. It will be an organization that has witnessed your community work firsthand and knows you to be a mover and shaker of the finest order. *They wish to honor you.*

You will accept, of course, with the initial denial that you have accomplished anything worthy of their attention. You are lying, of course. But you lay it on just enough to ensure *they believe you to be humble.*

When the appointed award ceremony comes, you cannot forget to thank a soul. Again, why deflect the attention away from you and onto those sorry posers? Because by so doing, you can enumerate each task you directed, and your accomplishment will seem even greater. Remember not to name them by name. They don't get any of your limelight. Just refer to them in the collective.

But we have gone over this before. Here is the real message of this chapter.

You will say, "The committee to eradicate adolescent vaping was such a worthwhile endeavor. I cannot count the *many* sleepless nights I spent strategizing over how to further this goal. I thank the sub-committee who tirelessly polled the student bodies of every public high school in Pasadena. [*Nod in their direction and wait for a polite clap.*] I thank the subcommittee of fine data sorters [*polite clap from the audience*], the subcommittee of vaping statistics [*another polite clap*], and the subcommittee of alternative substances [*another tiny clap because no one knows what that is, and you're not going to bother to explain it*]. I truly honor these tireless heroes.

"And I thank this community. I personally spent *every* waking moment calling politicians, educators, wealthy entrepreneurs, and clergy to gather endorsements. They did not disappoint me.

"I *personally* spoke to women's groups, men's clubs, and other community-minded organizations to solicit donations for our cause. In addition, I am proud to say we exceeded our expectations. EAV is now a fixture in *every* high school in our county. Our teenagers are finally protected!"

(*Pause here for wild clapping.*)

"It was a *monumental* sacrifice of my time and talents but what a reward to see these healthy young men and women, so full of promise, no longer addicted to something so destructive. I gratefully accept this coveted Golden Buffalo Award as a testament to what a community can do when we rally together!"

Anyone with any sense will be barfing in the aisles as you make your little self-honoring speech, but since those are not the circles in which you move, glide past it with your popularity intact.

39. Do Not Admit to Not Having Enough Time

Everyone who has had contact with you in the past will know that you are too busy for their childish family dinners, petty Tupperware parties, or other insignificant neighborhood soirees. They will know this because you have politely declined all invitations to their social functions—that is, those that do not deserve your presence. If the governor were to invite you for dinner, of course, you would accept. That increases your standing in the community.

As we discussed previously in chapter 27, you will decline the invitations that require you to actually interact rather intimately with those who are beneath you. There will be the odd dinner party that you simply cannot escape, however. An invitation from your daughter's best friend's family, for instance, is such an invitation. Although you would rather not go because, well, the intimacy issue. Sometimes it is better just to face the music and get it over with. Perhaps there is the odd direct sales jewelry party that your neighbor has asked you to join. Those parties can be very easy to deflect, though, by warning the hostess (while accepting the invitation) that you cannot stay but that you will pop in for a bit. Stay long enough to sit and chat politely before exiting without any purchase. She will be ever so grateful to have had you at all.

As a rule, people will begin to see you as someone who simply does not have time for such nonsense. That is a good thing because it keeps you above the human fray.

"But wait!" you say. This chapter is entitled "Do Not Admit to Not Having Enough Time." (And I stick by that title.) While it is important to give the impression you are too busy—too important, that is—for meaningless social functions, when you are offered an important speaking engagement, committee position, or other opportunity that would benefit your reputation, you must always accept. In this way, it will appear to others that you have unlimited time and resources. And when you accept, do it with the most graciousness you can muster without letting the hysteria behind your eyes show.

But, but, but. Why would you ever do this to yourself and what can be gained from it? As you must know by now, running committees is nothing but time-consuming. It is undoubtedly true that, at times, you will not have time to accept another new opportunity; a normal woman doing so would produce a mental breakdown, shrill interactions, or a frazzled appearance. How will you do it without reducing yourself to one of those nightmares?

First, recognize that every opportunity that comes your way furthers your popularity. If you already have too many positions to balance, simply find temporary substitutes for those that are possible to delegate. Make sure that you choose someone who is a bit inept so that by comparison, your committee will miss your leadership.

Second, remind your husband that he is owed vacation time from his office and press him into service for those positions that do not require your actual hands-on decision-making. Those positions, for example, would be something such as directing your minions to set up a school book faire or decorate for the high school prom. You will have to provide your husband with a schematic of what you expect and rehearse this phrase with him, "I know Margaret is much better at this than I am, but we are all intelligent people. We'll figure it out together." You, of course, have left nothing to chance. He is only saying those things to reinforce that you are the actual leader and are very good at directing. He knows exactly what needs to be done, but he must charm those ladies into believing that he is a helpless male and that they need to rally to save him. It works every time.

Third, hire a cook, cleaning person, gardener, chauffeur, babysitter, or anyone else that can remove you from your household duties, freeing your time to focus on the matter at hand. Some things are not necessary for you to execute personally. Keep your eyes on the prize.

And then relax. Do not betray that you are flustered or otherwise harried and so overloaded. Meditate. Use breathing exercises. Engage in any self-talk that calms you, then get to work with the business of working through this new opportunity.

Quiz

Oh, have we forgotten to administer a quiz for a while? Let us rectify that sad situation with a doozy. True or false.

a)   Attend every Tupperware party you can because it will garner the appreciation of your neighbors, and they will line up to be on your committee.

b)   Your husband can sub for you when you have too much to do.

c)   Your husband makes a better committee chair than you do.

d)   There is no shame in hiring a professional chef to feed your family.

e)   Giving the impression that you are flustered gives others the impression that you are always busy with something important.

f)   The devil is in the details, so you should never delegate the details of any project.

Answers.

a)   *False*

b)   *True*

c) *False (maybe true but irrelevant since he is not gunning for your job)*
d) *True (whatever it takes)*
e) *False! (And the whole point of this chapter. If you got this one wrong, please reread immediately.)*
f) *False (If you are well organized, any chimpanzee can direct the details of your project.)*

40. Do Not Divulge Personal Feelings or Faults— They Will Come Back to Bite You

By now, you should have an idea of your perfect self. It does not include real friendships. It does not worry itself with interpersonal relationships. It does not reduce itself to bringing every Jane home for dinner. Your perfect self is an enigma, a renaissance woman, a marvel. She embodies grace, dignity, and elegance, coupled with excellent leadership skills.

But make no mistake. She is not a friend to anyone.

That means you never talk about your family in anything but glowing terms. You do not so much as hint that your children sometimes fail to do their chores or speak sharply to you when tired or are not quite as bright as you had hoped. You never let on that your husband drinks a bit too much when he is out with colleagues on a Friday night or that he is quite rude when he must visit your mother or that he often cheats a bit on his golf game. Your family must appear as perfect as you have portrayed yourself as being. Why is this important?

Let us imagine that you have had two or three challenging committee meetings in one morning. Just as you are ready to go home and put your feet up, you get a phone call that your youngest is complaining of a bellyache and is resting in the nurse's office at her school. This is annoying because you failed to get enough sleep the night before because of your own bellyache. However, you smile sweetly to your committee and confess that you must excuse yourself a bit prematurely to pick up your child. For some reason, one of your committee cannot let go of her last point. She needs resolution before she will let you go. She drones on for several minutes until your last nerve is about to snap.

A normal woman would not only cut her short, but she would explain to the group that your family had been suffering from a bout of stomach flu and that your daughter was the latest victim. You might say how your spouse had brought home this bug from his latest fishing trip and that now you were all suffering because he just *had* to go with his buddies, even though it was very bad timing and *you* were due for a vacation, too, and you had *begged* him to postpone the trip. You might also indulge your sense of indignation with a bit of "isn't that just how men are, though, ladies?" Surely, you would get some chuckles and head nods and then leave the meeting properly vindicated.

Oh, but not you. Not the socially self-promoted you. You may not indulge your personal feelings in front of these ladies in the least. You cannot behave as a normal woman might.

As good as it would feel to engender the sympathies of your committee, your vindication would come at a price. All those women would go home and ponder on that incident because it was counter to everything they had ever heard from you. Then they would begin to challenge the view they previously had of your husband. Instead of feeling as though he, as the perfect specimen of a husband, deserves the most ideal woman they know, they will begin to question whether he is just like all husbands everywhere after all. Every time they interact with your husband, they will remember your complaint, and they will look at him under a microscope. Soon, they will find he has become less than perfect.

Once they go down that path, they will begin to question everything else you have built so far. They will mentally examine whether you are even who you purport yourself to be!

Soon, your entire operation will crumble into mediocrity in their minds.

What is worse than mediocrity to the socially aspirational? Nothing, unless it is also that soon, your husband—and by extension, you—will be the subject of gossip. Women who have felt threatened by your accomplishments will suddenly have fodder to fuel their own vindication. They will tell everyone you know that your husband is not perfect, or he would not have been so selfish. They will blab that you are a whiner and that your marriage is practically falling apart. Not only will you look mediocre, but—even worse—everyone you know might soon pity you.

Pitied!

This is serious business, so take it seriously and avoid sharing your private frustrations with anyone.

You simply tell them that your daughter is not feeling well and needs your attention. You leave the meeting in the charge of your lieutenant without stopping to listen to the droning pest and without tattling on your husband.

Have you learned your lesson? May I move on? (I'm sorry for treating you a bit harshly, but you simply cannot risk missing this particular lesson. It could undo months of work and may require you to move out of state.)

Quiz

No quiz. (I am far too shaken over the possibility that you nearly squandered all our hard work on one moment of weakness.)

41. Allow Others to Serve You

You are the most accomplished woman you know. You can lead a committee with your eyes closed. You can make a presentation with your hands tied behind your back. You can schmooze over the most hardened administrator, quell the most ardent detractor's comments, and enliven any crowd with your words of brilliant wisdom. You have arrived.

How does one sustain such clever leadership?

One way is to allow others to serve you. This will require a bit of dexterity on your part. On the one hand, you must appear as though you need nothing from your underlings but their undying servile devotion to your committee. On the other hand, it is advantageous to appear occasionally needy so that their loyalties extend to you personally. The operative word, here, is *occasionally*. And please do not try this until you are well established as the most accomplished woman you know. Otherwise, you may appear as legitimately weak and needy, possibly undermining all your hard work so far.

Why does this matter? It is because, my fair one, that will create the illusion that you are vulnerable, approachable, one of them. Throughout your entire social career, they have been thinking, *She has done so very much for our community, I must repay her somehow.* They may not have consciously thought it but even still, the thought was ruminating in their minds and hearts.

So do your best to generate a sizeable need. It cannot be simply a bellyache as that would (a) be temporary, (b) make you look like a crybaby, and (c) not conjure up the extent of the feelings that you are hoping to. The best is a grave illness since everyone is afraid of that. Your detractors even have respect for a grave illness.

The problem is you can't really make that happen to yourself. That is something over which you have little control. Bummer. (Although, if you do get a serious illness, use it to your full advantage in the method I describe below.)

And actually, if you can pull it off, you could feign an episode of a life-threatening illness, but that requires real cunning and the absolute cooperation of your family. Not many can actually do it well, and if you do it poorly, you will render yourself a true social pariah as women gossip about you ("Can you believe she would fake such a thing? How needy she must be!") That will get you pitied or hated faster than anything I know.

You will have to go for an injury. I am not suggesting that you throw yourself down a flight of stairs, but you could opt for a non-life-threatening surgical procedure. Something akin to a bunionectomy. Something that requires you to be bedridden and seemingly helpless is best.

You will announce your upcoming surgery with a party, of course. Invite as many women as your house can hold and play pin-the-scar-on-the-metatarsal, eat dogs-in-a-blanket, and have the women write long lovely well-wishes in your recovery book. Enjoy being the center of attention because, of course, that is the reason you made a party out of telling them about your surgery in the first place. Make sure they know the exact date your operation is scheduled. Make certain they know how many days you will be in bed.

If you play this right, they will be thinking, *She has done so much for me personally. I finally have that chance to repay her.* The women will be anticipating how they will be sure to drop by with flowers and/or baked goods. You might even casually express how proud you are of your twelve-year-old that she has learned how to make a simple dinner and is anxious to show your family how she can care for you while you cannot care for her. This will bring a tear to your associates' eyes and cause them to think that you will need dinners every night for at least a week. Someone will probably create a dinner calendar to facilitate such kindness.

Without too much fuss, you have just invented the social event of the season, placed your surgery front and center into the minds of everyone you know, and created an environment where women are practically fighting to see who can serve you best.

Your upcoming surgery will not bring the pity of others as in the last chapter. No. They will speak in glowing terms of your bravery and stoicism. This is what you want: to have others serve you but appear as though you don't actually need it. Logic will say that you need it, but your demeanor never will. They must believe that in spite of your surgery, you could, in a moment's notice, jump from your bed and organize a sit-down dinner for thirty guests for the day after tomorrow.

You have assured their loyalty to you forever.

42. Refer to Yourself in the Third Person

I used to think that it was a stupid violation of English grammar when people referred to themselves in the third person as in "Kathryn thinks this grammar usage is stupid." But then I took a look at the people who normally engage in this type of behavior. Charles De Gaulle, the former French prime minister did it. The British Queen Elizabeth routinely does it. And apparently, even some Americans, such as the former president Donald Trump and movie icon Kim Basinger, are known to have done it in magazine interviews.

What do these people have in common? I ask you. I will answer you, too. They are famous. It has not worked out too badly for these people, if you ask me. So why not give it a go?

Okay, I hear you saying that that isn't really a recommendation. You could probably site three additional famous people who trip people in restaurants, snort Jell-O every afternoon, or eat nachos for breakfast, but one should probably not follow those practices. So for all you naysayers, I will give you a solid reason for referring to yourself in the third person.

It conjures up the image of royalty.

That's it. This is just an extension of the Royal we that we discussed in chapter 30. Let's face it. We all have been conditioned to know that referring to oneself in the third person automatically causes the listener to think of that person as royalty and hold him/her in a higher regard. But because we are not, in point of fact, royalty, one must be a bit judicious when using the third person so as not to appear ridiculous or cause our loved ones to try to institutionalize us immediately because we are sporting a case of Napoleonic complex.

So one should never say, "Kathryn thinks that" or "Kathryn wants this." Especially if you have a common name such as mine (Kathryn), your listeners will merely think that you are referring to some other Kathryn/Catherine/Katherine. There are so many of us, after all. (Stupid beautiful but common name.) No, no. I could never let you make that mistake.

How this works best is always to use your last name in the plural. Here is example one.

> She will say, "We just love your family. We'd
> love to have you over for dinner on Friday."
> You will say, "Friday? Oh, I am so sorry. I
> believe the Latours are attending a gala on Friday."

In the above example, you must think of yourself as taking the place of the highly paid social secretary of a very busy famous person. It is your obligation to let people down gently when you are disappointing them. It is also your obligation to weed out the insignificant appointments as being beneath you, whether or not you actually have a gala to attend. The redeeming feature of this letdown procedure is the use of the third person. It makes it seem as though the matter is completely out of your hands. You do not look like the mother of a bunch of kids who could manipulate their calendars at will. Instead, you look like the nondecision maker of a very important group of people.

Example two is a slight twist on the first example because it asks for your opinion.

> She will ask, "What do you think about
> establishing a community center on Main Street?"
> You will say, "Actually, the Latours are
> strongly in favor of that idea."

All of a sudden, instead of a cozy, homey statement of what your cute little family likes, you have turned this into an elite family's opinion. Most people, when asked such a question, would say "We love it" or, even the more appropriate, "I think it's a great idea."

Occasionally, there will be a look of confusion and Ms. X will say, "No, I'm asking you what *you* think." You may then modify your statement to reflect that, of course, your opinion coincides with the Latour family's opinion. Somehow, when one lumps a whole family behind one's opinion, it becomes stronger. Never mind that you have no idea what your family's true opinion of the said issue is because they have never been asked about said issue because, frankly, no one cares what they think about said issue. Never mind that the woman who asked the question couldn't care less about what your family thinks about said issue.

However, because you have answered in this manner, suddenly, she has the full force of your family behind your opinion, making it that much stronger. More importantly, though, she realizes the appropriate social level on which your family resides, and it is—of course—a few notches above anyone else's.

In fact, it is on a par with royalty.

Quiz

Please answer these true or false.

a) It is appropriate to trip others in restaurants.
b) It is always okay to make people feel bad for daring to invite your family to dinner.
c) If someone asks for your opinion, tell her to go eat nachos for breakfast.

Answers:

a) *False*
b) *False*
c) *False*

(I knew you weren't paying attention. You got those all incorrect, didn't you? Ha! You can't fool me.)

43. Never Form Close Friendships but Make Everyone Feel as though They Are Your Special Friend

This might be the trickiest skill of all. Good luck with that. And on to the next chapter.

*****

I would never leave you like that. I would never do that to you. And the joke is on you anyway because this is the last chapter.

This is the crux of it all, after all. The *pièce de résistance.* If you learn no other thing from this book, learn this. You do not need people to be your friends. You cannot afford to have friends, or at least you cannot spend time generating new friends at this time of your life. Your social career must always come before real friendships, if any.

Repeat after me. "I will not care whether anyone actually likes me as long as they regard me as the most popular accomplished woman they know." This is your mantra. Repeat it often. Shall we do it now, together?

"I will not care whether anyone actually likes me as long as they regard me as the most popular accomplished woman they know."

Curl up in bed with it at night because that mantra—not actual human affection—will be what keeps you going in the dark hours. I mean, a husband and children are good to have, but other than those—oh, and your parents and siblings. Okay, mantra number two: No one who is not a family relation can have my true friendship.

Oh, and you can pretend that I am your friend if that makes you feel better.

Here is what you do. You do what I have already told you to do: Invite groups of people to your home but never just a special friend or one special family. Say kind things to others but never mean it. Never allow those kind words to infiltrate your stony, driven heart. Speak to others as if you were addressing a large group, complete with sound bites and other words of wisdom succinct enough to quote. Give credit to others in a general way so that they will think you like and appreciate them. Fawn over those who can increase your popularity. Ignore, except in the most basic human way, those who cannot be of service to your goal. Associate only with those who can do service to your goals. Send pithy notes with adjectives grouped in threes about whatever sorry accomplishment a member of your committee has done. Join or create exclusive clubs, events, and pastimes that elevate your standing in your community, then brag about them in a non-jealousy-inducing way.

Do all of the above, but never indulge yourself in a single confidence, bit of humorous gossip, unburdening of your soul, or confession of weakness. Do not do the things that bind you to another human by divulging traces of your ineptitude, telling humorous anecdotes that display any fault or failure, or truly connecting. Keep your emotions in check (unless it serves you in the moment to appear sincere). Keep your face and interactions pleasant at all times.

But (and here is the money part) *behave as though each person you meet is your trusted special friend.*

You do that by

- smiling while deeply looking into her eyes;
- touching her gently on the shoulder as she confides in you;
- saying flattering words to her in the most sincere manner conceivable;
- recognizing, whenever possible, her accomplishments (as long as doing so does not take away from your own);
- offering your gratitude in person and with special notes that overinflate and praise her work;
- graciously turning down all invitations to her home with such pathos that she truly becomes convinced you two would otherwise be best friends;
- smiling and excusing yourself if she attempts to confide a personal matter to you;
- in short, do all the normal things one might do to curry a friendship without any of the emotion, love, or expenditure of your personal time; and
- pretend, pretend, and pretend.

Well, I don't have to tell you. You have read the book.

Go forward, my friend, and conquer your community one "special friend" at a time.

AFTERWORD

I have the sense that you are hoping to hear some real-life examples of why this behavior makes me so angry. Or why I am able to see past the phony behaviors of these women who are social self-promoters when I have assured you that if you do it well, all women will adore you and honor your name.

The first answer to that question is, of course, that the women I know who do this are not able to mask their disdain for their minions and treat them as though they are inferior, thus betraying their false motives.

The second answer is that they have no true emotions and are able to promote themselves without feeling they are doing anything unfriendly in the process.

I think the third answer is the most accurate: Most people give others the benefit of the doubt. If someone behaves as though she is your friend, most of us don't question her motive. We expect that most people are as we are. If we say kind things, we genuinely mean them. And if you have only cursory contact with someone who is disingenuous but sounds friendly, you may not pick up on her actual motives.

That brings me to my own experiences and those of some friends.

I have known several good examples of self-promoters. I will share a few examples of how they behaved and why it irked me. *And why I have written this book as a form of therapy.*

Jacqueline and the Dinner Club

The first was a woman who was well versed in self-promoting. I will call her Jacqueline. (She did have a completely pretentious name, but it wasn't Jacqueline. Being sued for defamation is no laughing matter.) She put herself as the head of many a committee, forming many of them herself. She gave her children ridiculous names and taught them to be secretly snotty to their peers. Actually, she did most of the things I have addressed in this book. And she was completely adept at the charade. I actually might not have noticed that she was faking all her friendships, except that I became friends with a woman she snubbed.

It was during one of Jacqueline's fancy monthly members-only dinner parties. Jacqueline's rules forbade anyone else, save her elite friends and their children, to attend. As the children aged and married, her rules allowed the children's spouses also to join. (This became problematic as six friends times an average of four children is a lot of people to begin with. Add partners of said children, and well, you get the idea.)

As it turned out, one of the children married the son of my friend, so he trotted off monthly to this prestigious dinner party with his bride. One particular evening, he was about to leave for the dinner party when he realized his father and brothers had left his mother alone to go camping. He kindly invited her along with him, and she agreed to go.

She told me that there were more than raised eyebrows at her social violation. A number of people asked, quite rudely, why she was there. Jacqueline took her aside and ever so graciously informed her of the rules and asked that she not violate them again. Overall, it was a devastating experience, especially since these same people were fellow members of her congregation, had children who were friends with her sons, and worked alongside her in various community committees. Apart from this dinner party, all these people had treated her warmly. She believed they were true friends. Or so she had thought.

Anastasia and the Subcommittee Chair

Another friend recounted an incident where she was uninvited to participate in one of Anastasia's committees that prepared an annual event. Anastasia formed the committee anew each year but usually rolled over members who wished to continue. My artistically gifted friend had devoted years to this project as the head of a subcommittee, but she was getting older and slower. I believed her efforts were still vital, but one year, Anastasia decided that she needed new blood on her committee. She made a blanket decision—without informing any subcommittee heads—not to invite subcommittee heads who had held the position several years in a row. My friend waited for the usual invitation to join Anastasia at the annual kickoff meeting, which never came.

To make matters worse, Anastasia had asked me to be a subcommittee chair, and I asked my talented friend to assist me. I, not knowing of Anastasia's poor handling of this situation, thought this would be another chance for my friend and me to collaborate as I had been an assistant to my friend for the last five years. This made the situation between us awkward. Indeed, my friend was crushed and refused my offer.

I spoke to Anastasia and told her she had offended my friend. Anastasia went to her home with flowers and apologized. But although she flattered and spoke gloriously of my friend's past accomplishments, the damage had been done. Anastasia had skipped one vital step in taking the committee in a new direction and paid for it by losing the admiration of my friend.

I will tell one last anecdote and then you must be satisfied because I try to keep those incidents tamped way down inside me. It does not do my blood pressure any favor to recount the real-life events of social self-promoters who refused to befriend me in any meaningful way.

Maleficent and Her Tears

Another self-promoter who I will call Maleficent (again, it is no joke to be sued) had finagled her way into many lofty positions, had her husband invite her to speak at important functions, and had created accomplished children who did her bidding. She had even leveraged her serious illness into a sort of community event. In short, she was following the path of a true social self-promoter.

First, let me remind you that I cannot bear to practice the art of social self-promotion. I suppose promoting behavior I cannot stand is the epitome of hypocrisy, but I simply cannot behave as though I like someone when I have seen her behaving cruelly or in a fake manner. No. I curry real and enduring friendships, even though those friendships may not help my social career. Usually, I prefer those who cannot help me socially because they are people who I find more interesting. I actually enjoy them.

At some point, as with Jacqueline and Anastasia, I heard a friend complain about something Maleficent did that was hurtful, even though the friend admitted she herself was probably to blame. I also saw Maleficent do something ruthless to a friend in a "friendly" manner. These events caused me to rethink my "friendship" with Maleficent.

In my need to sort out who Maleficent was, I reexamined all my interactions with her. Although I had invited her family to dinner, she had never invited us. She had scheduled social events on top of my social events, depleting my attendance. She had sent me thank-you notes that were of the over-adjectived over-the-top variety. Adding up the sum total of our countless interactions, I suddenly saw that none of it had been sincere. There had been no real chumminess between us. She had never once actually reciprocated my genuine efforts to be her friend.

I stopped favorably responding to her fake smiles. I avoided her in hallways. I rejected her calls for help on committees.

One Sunday, after she had spoken to my congregation, I decided to speak to her. After all, she had given an almost-moving talk. I would be magnanimous and extend a genuine compliment. Isn't that what honorable people try to do? After I did so, she grabbed my hand and, with tears in her eyes, said, "I don't know what I've done to lose your friendship, but I hope you will try to be my friend again. Will you try?"

At that moment, I thought, *What friendship? When have you actually been a friend, and what exactly have you lost?* I suddenly understood that she had perfected the fine art of social self-promotion. Tears and a heartfelt plea? That was genius.

You can do the same. Go forth and be Maleficent.

ABOUT THE AUTHOR

 A Stanford-educated attorney who wonders why she ever went to law school, Kathryn Latour is first and foremost a *creatician*, and when found in her native habitat is hunched either over her sewing machine, a furniture sander, or a tube of glue. The mother of five extremely good-looking adults, Kathryn is an accomplished pianist/composer, party-thrower, and Dutchophile. Ever seeking the next adventure, she and her Euro husband have lived in California, Belgium, Pennsylvania, the Netherlands, and Portland. They traveled much of the world before Kathryn discovered that her favorite place was at home…by the fire…with a book.

CPSIA information can be obtained
at www.ICGtesting.com
Printed in the USA
LVHW020421170322
713568LV00007B/622